INSIDIOUS INTENT
AN INTERPRETATION
OF FEDOR SOLOGUB'S
THE PETTY DEMON

STUDIES OF
THE HARRIMAN INSTITUTE
COLUMBIA UNIVERSITY

INSIDIOUS INTENT
AN INTERPRETATION
OF FEDOR SOLOGUB'S
THE PETTY DEMON

Diana Greene

Slavica Publishers, Inc.

Slavica publishes a wide variety of textbooks and scholarly books on the languages, people, literatures, cultures, history, etc. of the USSR and Eastern Europe. For a complete catalog of books and journals from Slavica, with prices and ordering information, write to:

Slavica Publishers, Inc.
PO Box 14388
Columbus, Ohio 43214

ISBN: 0-89357-158-X.

This book was published in 1986.

Text set by Gail Lewis.

Printed in the United States of America.

328801

Streets that follow like an argument
Of insidious intent. . .

T. S. Eliot

For Joel

Contents

Acknowledgments

It is a pleasure to be able to thank publicly the people who made it possible for me to write this book.

Professor Robert Maguire, who was my dissertation adviser, has been a constant source of inspiration, encouragement and very constructive criticism in all stages of this work. Professors William Harkins, Marina Astman and James Coulter also gave me encouragement and valuable suggestions.

Lynn Solotaroff, editor and friend, helped me to refine significantly both the form and content of this work.

Professor Michael Wood kindly read an early version of Chapter 3, offered insights and helped me clarify my ideas about the European novel.

Thanks to Irene Balaksha, Marie Bienstock, Marina Khazanov, and Dmitry Mikheyev for advice on translation. Any mistranslations, of course, are mine.

The librarians at Columbia's Butler Library were invariably kind and helpful.

Part of this work was done with the help of a postdoctoral fellowship from the Russian Institute of Columbia University in 1979-80. An early version appeared in the *Ulbandus Review*, Spring, 1978.

Finally, I would like to thank Dr. Joel Berne, my husband, who sustained me through years of writing with faith, understanding, love and humor.

A Note On Transliteration

Throughout this text I have used the Library of Congress system to transliterate Russian words into English except that I have substituted a final "y" for "ii" at the end of such familiar names as Gorky, Bely and Dostoevsky. Also, in quoting from works that use other systems, I have kept the spelling of Russian words and names as they appeared.

Chapter 1
Introduction

The Petty Demon (*Melkii bes*), Fedor Sologub's strange but brilliantly original fin du siècle novel, concerns the growing insanity of Peredonov, a sadistic, provincial *gimnaziia* teacher. Peredonov wants so much to achieve his greatest ambition—to become a school inspector—that his mistress, Varvara, easily tricks him into marrying her; she simply forges two letters from an influential princess promising Peredonov the inspectorship if he marries Varvara. A contrasting subplot details the erotic but unconsummated affair between Aleksandr (Sasha), one of Peredonov's students, and Liudmila, a decadent young woman. In the course of the novel the two stories alternate with increasing rapidity and finally converge in a grand finale at a costume ball. Sasha, dressed as a Japanese geisha, wins the prize and barely escapes an enraged mob, while Peredonov, by then in the grip of madness, sets fire to the hall. Shortly after, when he finds that Varvara has duped him, he loses his sanity entirely and murders Volodin, his closest friend. Sasha and Peredonov go their separate ways—Peredonov to the madhouse, Sasha to adulthood—the reader being left to speculate on the relationship between the two.

First published in its entirety in 1907, *The Petty Demon* delights and annoys readers as intensely today as it did when it first appeared. Indeed, recent translations of the novel into several European languages, and even into Japanese, attest to an increasing and broadening readership. One would hardly have expected this work to attract new generations of readers, however, for in content it revolves around political and aesthetic problems of the 1890s, and in form it stands as an unrepeated experiment, a cul de sac in the evolution of the novel genre. What is it about *The Petty Demon* that has enabled it to transcend its own turbulent times and speak so powerfully to ours?

An attempt to answer this question raises several difficulties which are complicated by the novel's long gestation period and unusual publication history. Sologub started working on *The Petty*

Demon in 1892 and finished it ten years later. It was not until 1905, however, that the novel began to be serialized in Dmitrii Merezhkovsky and Zinaida Gippius' journal, *Voprosy zhizni* (*Questions of Life*) and even then it was ignored because the journal ceased publication before the entire novel could be printed.[1] In 1907, five years after the novel's completion, *Shipovnik* publishing house finally brought out *The Petty Demon* in book form and this time it caused a furor that continued for many years. Sologub was forced to retire early from his post as a school inspector (it is not clear whether the authorities objected to the eroticism of the Sasha-Liudmila subplot or to Sologub's depiction of a *gimnaziia*), while at the same time he suddenly became very famous. Indeed, shortly thereafter Nikolai Gumilev opened a review by observing sourly that "Sologub has written a lot but perhaps even more has been written about him so that it may be superfluous to write about him again."[2] However, the fifteen years that had elapsed between the inception of *The Petty Demon* and its belated recognition had been a time of dramatic historical and literary events in Russia. Thus, before we can discover the qualities that have allowed this novel to endure, it will be necessary to place it in a rather complicated historical and literary context, one that includes not only relevant events of the 1880s, but also the development of the Russian symbolist movement, as well as changes in the novel genre at the end of the nineteenth century.

Because *The Petty Demon* is set in a provincial backwater at the end of the nineteenth century, characters and situations in the novel reflect the extremely repressive political climate that dominated Russia from the 1880s. In fact, *The Petty Demon* makes a sardonic comment on the era of political reaction which started in 1881, when terrorists assassinated Alexander II, the reluctant liberator of the serfs.[3] Even Russia's economic gains—the accelerating industrialization and railroad building that continued up to the Revolution—in no way affected the prevailing political climate of gloom, repression and apathy. In an article entitled "The Despondency and Pessimism of Contemporary Educated Society" which appeared in 1885 in the then populist journal *Severnyi vestnik* (*The Northern Herald*) a Professor Ivanov described the despair of the intelligentsia and linked it (as explicitly as he dared) with the repressive regime of Alexander III:

> Despondency and pessimism nowadays are present in all phenomena of the human spirit; they manifest even more clearly in those fields where the human spirit can express itself most intensively and fully, i.e., in belles lettres and philosophy. Statistics demonstrate an omnipresent and constantly increasing use of alcohol . . . . the number of suicides is increasing everywhere.[4]

The author attributes the despondency and pessimism of his age to "a deep discord between our world view and the forms of our personal and societal life . . . between ideas about the rights of man [the principle of equality before the law] and [actual] societal relations." He writes that it is impossible, as some would like, to go back to the Middle Ages when people considered "all the surrounding institutions completely necessary and fair . . . . Adults can, of course, regret the joys of childhood, but once childhood is gone, it is gone forever and no force of will can return it. Similarly, it is just as impossible for contemporary educated man to make himself into a man of several hundred years ago." The solution to man's present unhappiness, the writer believes, lies in the defeudalization of Russia, the narrowing of the economic and social gaps between the supposedly free serf and the intelligentsia, or, as he more obliquely puts it,

> the creation of institutions in which all citizens would be provided in reality, and not just on paper, with the possibility of participating in the benefits of the culture . . . . There is only one way out—a movement forward toward the realization of the basic contemporary idea that all citizens have the right to equal happiness and to the wealth of a progressive culture. And the steadier, more consistent and energetic this movement is, the quicker the moral pain of contemporary educated humanity will disappear.

Although Sologub undoubtedly shared Ivanov's views, he expressed them very differently; whereas Ivanov criticized the government directly (though very cautiously), in *The Petty Demon* Sologub took a more oblique approach and exaggerated to the point of parody the ultra-reactionary policies of Alexander III and his advisers, principally the notorious archconservative Konstantin Pobedonostsev (1827-1907). Pobedonostsev's ideas made a fitting subject for satire—he loathed constitutional government, universal suffrage and political parties, thought that knowledge was the root of all evil, and believed that only through the institutions of the state, the Russian Orthodox Church, and the patriarchal family could Russia be saved.[5]   Unfortunately, he wielded enormous power, and his reactionary views and dour personality stamped the reigns of both Alexander III (1881-1894) and Nicholas II (1894-1917).   Not only did he act as tutor to the last two Romanovs, but as Ober-Procurator of the Holy Synod from 1880 to 1905 ("the eye of the tsar" in the church, as Peter the Great described that position), he enjoyed unlimited power over ritual, dogma, education of the clergy, indeed, all Christian education (including parish schools), and church property.   In a country with a national religion, this influence extended to social legislation, civil rights and control of citizens' access to information.   Moreover, from the start, Pobedonostsev insisted on being included in the tsar's Council of Ministers, thus helping to determine all internal affairs and gaining virtual control over the appointment of governors and ministers.[6]   He used his power to limit the freedom of all nonRussian people and all religions except Russian Orthodoxy, and to keep the lower classes as ignorant as possible. Ironically, Pobedonostsev's rigid, autocratic and unjust policies helped to make the revolution he so feared inevitable.

In the field of education, however, Pobedonostsev exercised perhaps his greatest and most baleful influence.   Because D. A. Tolstoy, the previous Ober-Procurator, had for fourteen years simultaneously served as Minister of Education—with profound and unpleasant consequences for academic freedom in the Russian educational system—Pobedonostsev inherited great power not only over parochial schools but also over all secular schools including universities.   Although Alexander III on ascending the throne in 1881 nominally separated the two offices by appointing a new Minister of Education, the choice of Count Ivan Delianov for this post was Pobedonostsev's and thus the Ober-Procurator's control over all education remained virtually unchallenged.   Indeed, Delianov's complete cooperation with the Ober-Procurator earned him the title of "Pobedonostsev's henchman."[7]

The stultifying educational policies Pobedonostsev enacted (and by implication his other policies as well) came under attack in Sologub's novel, which appropriately concerns a provincial *gimnaziia*.   No doubt Sologub who himself taught math for many years in such *gimnazii* had experienced the oppressive effects of

Pobedonostsev's policies at first hand and so made them his special target. It seems likely, however, that he further regarded the educational policies (which were perfectly consonant with the rest of Pobedonostsev's social and political program) as representative of governmental policy in general. Thus Sologub may have used a school setting to make the injustices of the regime stand out more sharply since here the victims were children.

How, then, did Sologub use satire to attack the government's educational policies and also suggest more sweeping criticisms of the regime? In general, he poked fun at the government by having his characters voice, bluntly and explicitly, attitudes that officials usually sugar-coated or only implied. Pobedonostsev, for example, strongly believed that social mobility through education should not be permitted, an opinion he may have expressed privately to Alexander III and allowed to influence school regulations, but certainly one he never promulgated publicly. In Sologub's novel, however, this opinion is endorsed openly and enthusiastically (and with very humorous effect) by both the authoritarian and choleric town prosecutor and the increasingly insane protagonist, Peredonov:

> "Heredity is a great thing!" the prosecutor screamed ferociously. "To turn peasants into aristocrats is stupid, ridiculous, wasteful and immoral. The land is impoverished, the city fills with tramps, there are crop failures, ignorance, suicides. Is that what you want? Teach a peasant as much as you like, but don't give him a rank for it."[8]

The prosecutor is alluding to the fact that graduates of *gimnazii*, no matter what social class they had come from originally, were granted certain upper-class privileges: they were given the first of fourteen government ranks established by Peter the Great, and the opportunity through advancement to become members of the nobility, or even hereditary members; they were exempted from being drafted into the infantry (no small benefit as the term of conscription was twenty-five years until 1874 and six years thereafter); and they were eligible for a university education. In *The Petty Demon* the prosecutor views such mobility with fear and abhorrence and expresses himself unambiguously on the subject:

"The peasantry is losing its best members and will eternally remain rabble and riff-raff, and the nobility will also suffer harm from the flood of lower-class elements. In his own village he [the peasant who goes to a *gimnaziia*] was better than the others, but he will bring to the upper class something crude, unchivalrous, ignoble. His first concern is with profit and his own stomach. No, old man, the castes were wisely established." (146)

By "castes" the prosecutor means the system of legal estates (*sostoianiia* or *sosloviia*) which were codified in the eighteenth century and which endured, with some modification, up to the Revolution. The estate into which one was born—noble, clerical, urban (merchants and petty bourgeoisie), peasant or Cossack—determined one's rights and obligations in relation to the tsar. Movement from one estate to another (for example, a peasant child being allowed to enter a *gimnaziia*) although possible was made very difficult. Sologub, who was born into the poorest stratum of urban life but who managed to become a teacher and later a very wealthy writer, has Peredonov in *The Petty Demon* loudly complain to the prosecutor that the *gimnaziia* director compromises the caste system by letting middle- and lower-class children into the school:

> "And our director allows all kinds of trash into our *gimnaziia*," Peredonov said angrily. "There are even peasant children and even more petty bourgeois."
> "That's a fine state of affairs," screamed his host.
> "There's a circular not to allow any riff-raff in, but he does what he wants," complained Peredonov. "He refuses almost no one. 'In our town,' he says, 'it's cheap to live, and,' he says, 'there are so few *gimnaziia* students.' So what if there are few? Let there be even fewer! It's all you can do even to keep up with correcting the homework." (146-147)

The circular Peredonov refers to was probably the infamous "Cooks' Children" decree of June 1887, issued by Education Minister Delianov with the full support of Alexander III and the help of Pobedonostsev. This unapologetic assertion of law and order and the interests of the state over the needs and potentials of individuals has, at least, the virtue of candor:

Gymnasiums and progymnasiums are freed from receiving the children of coachmen, servants, cooks, launderers, small tradesman and the like, whose children, with the exception, perhaps, of those who are gifted with extraordinary capacities, ought by no means be transferred from the sphere to which they belong, and thus brought, as many years' experience has shown, to slight their parents, to feel dissatisfied with their lot, and to conceive an aversion to the existing inequality of fortune, which is in the nature of things unavoidable.[9]

The decree caused an uproar as well as a great deal of resentment[10] and the above citations from *The Petty Demon* show that Sologub, who was teaching at the time, must have been affected by this arbitrary limiting of educational opportunities for the poor. He was, after all, the son of a tailor and a housemaid who only received his education—at a pedagogical institute—through the generosity of his mother's employers.

A second important educational policy with political overtones that Sologub criticizes in the novel is the lifeless *gimnaziia* curriculum, which was standard throughout the country and designed to inculcate patriotism, religion, and a veneration for antiquity while stifling original (considered synonymous with revolutionary) thought. In the course of the novel we see Peredonov, who is a literature teacher in the *gimnaziia*, discuss works by Pushkin (1799-1837) and Krylov (1769-1844) but nothing more modern. The boredom this curriculum engenders can be seen from the way Sasha, a student, dismisses his school work as quickly as possible the one time his friend Liudmila brings it up:

"Latin and Greek," said Liudmila, "How sick you must be of them!"

"No, not at all," Sasha answered, but it was obvious that already, just talking about textbooks was evoking in him the usual boredom. "It's rather boring to cram, but it doesn't matter—I have a good memory. But I do like doing math problems." (233)

The curriculum in the *gimnazii* was, indeed, limited. As early as 1866 D. A. Tolstoy, then Minister of Education, decreed that "the education of young people has to be conducted in the spirit of religion, respect for private property, and observance of the fundamental principles of public order." The curriculum for

gimnazii established by the Ministry of Education in 1871 and
effective until 1890 tried to implement this principle by adding four
hours a week of Greek, four of math, removing two hours of
history and replacing much literature with Old Church Slavonic.
In the seven-year *gimnaziia* program religion accounted for three
hours a week, Latin for forty-nine, and Greek for thirty-six! Two
years before Sologub began writing his novel the curriculum was
modified to add three hours a week of religion, eliminate seven
hours of Latin and three of Greek.[11]   Those who revised the
curriculum apparently de-emphasized science, history and any
literature after Pushkin, because they felt that these were
politically dangerous subjects.   Perhaps they feared science because
they saw it replacing the authority of the church and state with
that of the trained observer, i.e., the *intelligént.*   At any rate,
science seems to have been a symbol of freedom of thought for
radicals of the 1860s and '70s, many of whom studied physiology
and medicine (like the dozens of women who left Russia to study
medicine in Zurich in the '70s and then returned to join
revolutionary parties[12]).   Bazarov, the controversial frog-dissecting
hero of Turgenev's *Fathers and Sons,* illustrated and even proved
for some people the connection between the study of natural
sciences and radical thought.   History, literature and philosophy
had, in the hands of the radical critics of the '60s, become
metaphors for political discussions critical of the government and
thus also were frowned upon.   In describing Sasha's boredom in
school Sologub shows how the abstract curriculum developed by the
government to discourage rebelliousness in students also stunted
their mental growth.   Only mathematics—the subject least affected
by politics—retains any interest for Sasha.

     Still another educational policy which Sologub attacks was the
government's blatant discrimination against *zemstvo* schools and its
promotion of church schools.   *Zemstvos* were the peasant assemblies
which administered local services including primary education.
Although the power to veto all *zemstvo* decisions was held by the
Marshal of the Nobility, at this time the *zemstvos* were felt to be a
possible source of political unrest because they were considered too
powerful.   Consequently, in 1889 land captains, responsible to the
Ministry of the Interior, were instated to supervise *zemstvo*
decisions.   Furthermore, because *zemstvo* schools were considered
too liberal in orientation, as of 1885 Pobedonostsev tried to
establish a competing parochial school in each parish.   These parish

schools, run by the local priest, concentrated on religious piety and taught only minimal literacy. By 1891 a decree required *zemstvos* to apply to church authorities for permission to open a school and such permission was often denied on the grounds that there already was a church school in the area. In *The Petty Demon* Peredonov embarrasses Aleksandr Mikhailovich Veriga, the Marshal of the Nobility and president of the *zemstvo* assembly by crudely expressing his dislike for the *zemstvo* schools. Veriga shares Peredonov's opinion, but because he wishes to become governor, feels he must maintain a semblance of impartiality. He therefore responds to Peredonov with a long-winded speech full of bureaucratic jargon that in substance repeats Peredonov's ideas. In reality, Peredonov and Veriga represent two aspects of the government—Peredonov, the underlying prejudices and Veriga, the hypocritical rhetoric. Veriga says:

> "Look, you're a pedagogue, and because of my position in the district I have to deal with schools as well. From your point of view, which school, pray, would you give preference to: the parochial parish, or these so-called local [*zemstvo*] ones?" . . .

> Peredonov scowled, looked from corner to corner, and said, "The local schools need to be improved."

> "Improved," Veriga repeated in an undefined tone, "just so." And he lowered his eyes to his disintegrating cigar as if preparing to hear a long explanation.

> "The men teachers there are nihilists," said Peredonov, "and the women teachers don't believe in God. They stand in church and blow their noses . . . . In their schools they are very free," Peredonov continued. "There isn't any discipline. They don't want to punish them at all. But you can't treat peasant children like those of the nobility. They need to be whipped."

> Veriga calmly looked at Peredonov; then, as if feeling uncomfortable because of the tactless blunder he had heard, he lowered his eyes and said in a cold tone, almost that of a governor:

> "It must be said that I have observed many good qualities in the pupils of rural schools. Undoubtedly in the vast majority of cases they have a completely conscientious attitude toward their work. Of course, as

with children everywhere, misbehavior occurs. As a result of the ill-breeding that surrounds them, this misbehavior can take rather crude forms, all the more so because in the rural population of Russia the feelings of duty and honor and respect for others' property are undeveloped. The school is obligated to deal with such misbehavior attentively and strictly. If all measures of reprimand are exhausted, or if the misbehavior is great, then, of course, it would be necessary to resort to extreme measures in order not to expel the boy. However, this relates to all children, even to the nobility. But in general, I agree with you that in schools of this type the education offered is not completely satisfactory." (152–154)

Another repressive educational practice that Sologub satirized in the novel was the inspection of students' lodgings to determine if they were sufficiently respectable, a practice that was started in 1845 and revived in 1871 under D. A. Tolstoy.[13] In the novel Peredonov, who dreams of becoming a school inspector, decides to strengthen his candidacy by making impromptu inspections of students' homes. During these visits he not only inspects the lodgings, but intimidates the parents or guardians, complains about the student's behavior, and then demands that the student be beaten, a demand often acted upon. Peredonov enhances his sadistic enjoyment by bragging about his exploits in class the next day in front of his discomforted victim.

Sologub uses his hateful protagonist to extend his satire of governmental attitudes and practices beyond educational issues. He attacks official bigotry when, in a conversation with Marta, a young Polish woman, he has Peredonov echo Pobedonostsev's attitudes toward Poles, Jews, and Russians:

> "Well, and are you going to revolt soon?"
>
> "Why revolt?" Marta said.
>
> "You're Poles, after all you're always planning to revolt, only it does no good."
>
> "I don't even think about that," said Marta. "And none of us wants to revolt."
>
> . . . .
>
> "We know how you don't think. Only we will not give your Poland back to you. We conquered you.

We did so many good things for you, but it's clear that
no matter how much you feed a wolf he always looks
toward the forest."

Marta did not protest. Peredonov was silent for a
while and suddenly said, "Poles have no brains."

Marta blushed. "Anyone can be that way—Russians
or Poles."

"No, it's really so, it's true," Peredonov insisted.
"Poles are stupid. They only give themselves airs.
Now Yids, they're clever . . . . Yids are a very clever
race . . . . A Yid will always swindle a Russian but a
Russian will never swindle a Yid . . . . Yids are clever
at everything, both in studies and in general. If they
let Yids be professors, all the professors would be Yids.
But Polish women are all slobs . . . .   Russians   are
imbeciles—all they ever invented was the samovar and
nothing else." (116-118)

Peredonov's outrageous crudeness and bigotry are only a slight
exaggeration of Pobedonostsev's actual opinions and of official
government policy. Pobedonostsev's rabid anti-Catholicism led him
to believe that all of the predominantly Catholic Poles were agents
of the Church and hostile to Russia. Disliking Poles on their own
account as well, Pobedonostsev enthusiastically continued the policy
of Russification that had been imposed on the Poles after their
unsuccessful revolt of 1863. Indeed, under Pobedonostsev the Poles
may have fared even worse than they did during the revolt; he
replaced the Polish language with Russian for all official purposes
and reinstated a decree issued during the Polish Revolt which
forbade people of Polish extraction to transfer land by purchase,
mortgage or lease. Although this decree had remained on the
books, it had been ignored for many years, but now all land
transfers made by Poles after 1863 were declared null and void,
reducing many families to poverty.[14]

Pobedonostsev's fear and hostility was even more pronounced
in relation to Jews, who, he felt, were all foreign agents and
revolutionaries, as well as the master-minds behind the liberal
press, libeling Russia both at home and abroad. In 1887
Pobedonostsev was instrumental in issuing a decree which restricted
Jews' access to higher education by establishing Jewish quotas in
gimnazii and universities. These quotas were ten percent in the
Pale of Settlement (the Southwest area of Russia where most Jews

were forced to live) and five percent elsewhere except in the most desirable Moscow and St. Petersburg universities, where the quota was three percent. The government, like Peredonov, seems to have felt that if too many Jews were educated, Russians would suffer. Nor was Pobedonostsev's opinion of Russians very flattering. He believed that "inertness and laziness are generally characteristic of the Slavonic nature" and for this reason he believed Russians needed firm religious and political guidance.[15] There was, however, a certain amount of subterfuge and hypocrisy about these governmental attitudes and policies. Pobedonostsev denied vehemently in the foreign press that Jews were persecuted in Russia, and Alexander III never took the final step of categorically denying the lower classes access to *gimnazii*, because he was afraid that the resulting furor abroad might harm Russia's foreign credit.[16]

Even more pervasive than bigotry was the general climate of political terror and denunciations that Pobedonostsev created in the '80s and early '90s and this, too, evokes Sologub's criticism and satire in the novel. Sologub suggests the unhealthiness of the political climate by having Peredonov, as he goes mad, become increasingly obsessed with denouncing others and with fears of being denounced. In a scene of wonderful deadpan humor, Veriga, the Marshal of the Nobility mentioned above, encourages Peredonov to confess the liberal sins of his political past while Peredonov, an extreme reactionary, as we have seen, insists fearfully that even during his younger "liberal" days he was an exemplary conservative:

> "So you were a great liberal," Veriga asked with a gracious smile. "You wanted a constitution, didn't you? We all wanted a constitution in our youth. Admit it."
>
> . . .
>
> "Of course, your excellency," Peredonov confessed. "I was at the university also, but even then I didn't want the same kind of constitution as others."
>
> "Specifically?" Veriga asked with a hint of approaching displeasure in his voice.
>
> "I wanted a constitution, only I wanted one without a parliament," Peredonov explained, "because in a parliament they only fight."
>
> Veriga's gray eyes were lit with quiet ecstasy. "A constitution without a parliament," he said dreamily. "You know, that's practical."

"But even that was a long time ago," said Peredonov, "and now I don't want anything." (151–152)

The novel's political implications were perhaps best understood and expressed by the Marxist critic P. A. Kogan who saw in Peredonov a model citizen of his time, one who embodied the effects of unremitting political oppression. Kogan writes:

Peredonov does not suffer because he is constrained on all sides; he is not only reconciled to this constraint but reveres it. He suffers because he thinks he is not clever enough to understand the significance of these constraints and therefore, not worthy to administer them. Peredonov suffers not because he is a slave but because he imagines that he does not fulfill the responsibility of a slave well enough.[17]

Kogan's insights into Peredonov's character are quite trenchant (as are some of his other remarks, to which we will return), and certainly, the allusions in the novel to the events and attitudes of the day merit some clarification. *The Petty Demon*, however, is far more than a political satire, and cannot be accounted for solely in historical and political terms. Clearly, the novel must be examined in a literary context as well.

The assassination of Alexander II which so constrained political life in Russia, naturally, had an equally serious effect on literature; in the subsequent crackdown, literary publications were severely curtailed. Just how severely curtailed can be gathered from an exchange in 1881 between Pobedonostsev and Nikolai P. Ignat'ev, Minister of the Interior. In answering a complaint about the unruliness of the press, Ignat'ev protested that he had already closed down more than fifty newspapers and journals. In August 1882 he wrote that he would like to ban all newspapers, but that both he and Pobedonostsev knew this would be impossible. That year a series of new censorship regulations were enacted to keep politically suspect people from working on newspapers or periodicals and to give the government the power to suspend any editor or publication.[18] Many journals were affected, most notably the prestigious and populist *Otechestvennie zapiski* (*Fatherland Notes*), which was closed in 1884. The satirist Saltykov-Shchedrin and the poet Nekrasov had been its editors. The immediate effect of these bannings was to leave fewer outlets for writers, but the long-term effects were far more harmful: writers and editors became more self-conscious and fearful and began to censor themselves. Civic themes became the order of the day.

This is not to suggest that there was no great literature in Russia in the 1880s. In this decade Chekhov published eight books of short stories and Garshin five, including his famous "Red Flower" (1885). Another short story writer, Korolenko, was prolific during this time as well, producing seven volumes, including "Makar's Dream" (1885). Tolstoy not only published his famous short stories "The Death of Ivan Il'ich" (1886) and "The Kreutzer Sonata" (1890), but wrote a play, The Power of Darkness (1886) and started working on his novel Resurrection. Among the poets, Fet produced some of his best work in Evening Fires of '83, '84, '89 and '91. Nadson and Apukhin, now lesser-known poets, were highly esteemed and very prolific at this time. Compared to the vast quantity of great Russian literature produced in the '60s and '70s, however, this represented a severe decline. Significantly, too, the '60s and '70s produced most of the great Russian novels—Turgenev's On the Eve and Fathers and Sons, Tolstoy's War and Peace and Anna Karenina, Dostoevsky's Crime and Punishment, The Idiot, The Devils and The Brothers Karamazov, and Saltykov-Shchedrin's The Golovlovs—but no great novels appeared in the '80s; the most notable works were short stories, plays and poetry, a trend that continued through the '90s and the first decade of the twentieth century.

Several reasons may be advanced for the decline of the panoramic, philosophical, realistic Russian novel in the '80s. First, and most obviously, the great masters of the Russian novel had fallen silent. Dostoevsky died in 1881, Turgenev in 1883 and Tolstoy repudiated his great novels in his Confession (written in 1879 and published three years later). The younger writers of the '80s preferred shorter literary forms. This, however, merely begs the question why these writers did not produce novels.

From one point of view it is possible that the discursive, speculative Russian novel of the '60s and '70s could not survive the stifling political atmosphere and gloom of the '80s; that the threat of censorship—always more effective than censorship itself—inhibited writers and made it impossible for them to express themselves and their social observations in this genre. Consequently, writers may have turned to shorter, more focused, and less ambitious forms because they were safer. On the other hand, it may be that the genre itself had been exhausted. The Soviet critic, Iurii N. Tynianov, takes an evolutionary viewpoint and posits that the novel, like other genres during earlier periods, had developed and expanded as far as possible. When, inevitably, the novel genre began to crumble under its own weight, it yielded to shorter, more vital forms, those more closely connected to everyday life.[19]

Whatever factors initiated the growth of short forms in the '80s, they were sustained and nourished by the change in world view that accompanied Russia's rapid industrialization in the '90s. John Cournos, Sologub's English translator, felt that changes in Russian society, especially the growth of transportation and communication at this time, made short forms more natural:

> Rapid transportation and intercommunication, the extreme restlessness, nervousness and "artificiality" of our age, the hurried way of living affected the Russian writer in this wise: he ceased to see life broadly in panoramic sweeps; he began to see it swiftly rather than thoroughly, as a series of impressions rather than as a whole: a thing of fragments.[20]

The effect of Russia's modernization on audiences as well as on writers also should be considered. In response to the factory jobs now available many people moved from the country to the cities. Short stories began appearing in newspapers for this growing proletarian audience while both the interest in and quality of novels fell off.

Just as both political and literary activity had decreased in the early 1880s, so in the early '90s both suddenly seemed infused with new energy. Expressions of political discontent rose dramatically. In 1887 a plot to assassinate Alexander III was uncovered (one of the conspirators who was hanged was Aleksandr Ul'ianov—Lenin's older brother), and the political situation was not improved when, in response to widespread famine and cholera in 1891 and '92, the government not only failed to help, but even denied the existence of the problem and actually banned voluntary organizations trying to provide relief for the hungry and dying. So great an outcry resulted that private organizations were eventually allowed to function. The disturbances became increasingly widespread and serious: strikes increased sharply in the '90s, including one by 30,000 St. Petersburg textile operators in 1896; student unrest also grew, fed by the brutality of the mounted police and the governmental policy of drafting into the army students who participated in demonstrations. Finally, the Social-Revolutionaries, the successors of the Populists, began a series of terrorist attacks on high government officials. In 1901 the Minister of Education was mortally wounded and an attempt was made to assassinate Pobedonostsev himself.

In literature, the sudden upsurge of energy that began in the early 1890s continued for about twenty-five years before subsiding on the eve of World War I and the Russian Revolution. This period is known as the Silver Age of Russian literature, a time of literary exuberance and creativity considered second in quality only to the Golden Age of Pushkin's time; *The Petty Demon*—begun at the dawn of symbolism, finished just as the movement was gathering momentum and published in its entirety at the height of the symbolist movement—stands both as the product of, and a monument to, a greater part of this era.

Starting in the early 1890s the literature of this period gradually divided into two tendencies which I will roughly characterize as neo-realistic and neo-romantic.[21] Writers of the first group saw themselves as the continuation of the realistic tradition of Tolstoy, Turgenev, and Goncharov, at least as interpreted by the utilitarian critics of the mid-nineteenth century—the most famous of whom were Vissarion Belinsky, N. G. Chernyshevsky, and N. A. Dobroliubov. These critics believed that art was no more than a reflection of life and therefore inferior to it, a doctrine expressed in its most extreme form in Dmitrii Pisarcv's famous statement that a good pair of boots is worth more than a play by Shakespeare. The purpose of art, they felt, was to help effect social change, and they used criticism of such works as *Fathers and Sons*, Goncharov's *Oblomov*, and Ostrovsky's *The Storm* as occasions for discussing what was wrong with Russia. Their successors, the neo-realists, also believed that art should serve a social purpose. Maksim Gorky, whose stories about tramps and other disenfranchised and disillusioned people won him great popularity in the '90s, was the leader of a group which included Aleksandr Ivanovich Kuprin, Leonid Nikolaevich Andreev, Aleksandr Serafimovich (Popov), and Vladimir Galaktionovich Korolenko, as well as less politically oriented writers such as Ivan

Aleksieevich Bunin and Anton Chekhov. For this group of writers—the "revolutionary school of fiction"—who gathered around Gorky's Moscow *Sreda* (Wednesday) literary circle and later found an outlet for their work in Gorky's *Znanie* publishing house—literature represented a weapon for social reform.[22]

The second, and for our purposes more important, neo-romantic, stream, the one to which Sologub belonged, was decadence, or symbolism as it came to be called, and included among its members Valerii Briusov, Konstantin Bal'mont, D. S. Merezhkovsky, Zinaida Gippius, Aleksandr Blok, Andrei Bely and Viacheslav Ivanov. This self-conscious and theatrical literary movement came to Russia with appropriate deliberateness and fanfare. In 1892 D. S. Merezhkovsky, in his famous essay, "O prichinakh upadka i o novykh techeniiakh sovremennoi russkoi literatury" ("Concerning the Decline of and New Currents in Contemporary Russian Literature"), expressed a general dissatisfaction with Russian literature while reinterpreting Russian writers such as Turgenev and Dostoevsky as unconscious symbolists. In 1894-1895 Valerii Briusov, a gifted and ambitious young poet who rightly thought that bringing the decadent movement to Russia would make him famous, published three pamphlets entitled *Russkie simvolisty* (Russian Symbolists). These were provocatively erotic and enigmatic symbolist poems, written chiefly by Briusov himself but published under different pen names to give the impression that symbolism was already an established movement. The collections enjoyed (in all senses of the word) a *succès du scandale*.[23] A. Volynskii (A. L. Flekser) further helped the movement when, starting in 1892, he wrote a series of articles about decadence and symbolism for *The Northern Herald* and convinced its publisher and editor, Liubov' Gurevich, to publish works by Gippius, Bal'mont, Sologub, and other symbolists through the '90s.[24] In 1898 Sergei Diagilev founded *Mir iskusstva* (*The World of Art*), a luxurious journal devoted to symbolist and religious-philosophical writing which, perhaps in an attempt to create a Wagnerian union of the arts, also featured art work by Vrubel', Somov, Levitan and Serov. Symbolist journals quickly proliferated and the movement was launched.

The Russian neo-realists had far less trouble defining their movement than did the Russian symbolists, for whom it became a major preoccupation. Nor is this surprising. While the neo-realists could feel themselves part of a long Russian literary tradition, the symbolists were constantly explaining and defending their movement, which to a large extent was self-created, self-conscious, and self-defined. In the course of his career as a symbolist Sologub himself was to write several articles on the subject.[25] Defining symbolism was no easy task because the symbolists borrowed their models and ideas from many different sources. They were inspired by Nietzsche, Ibsen, and Wagner; they admired Poe, Wilde, and the French symbolists; but they also claimed to have forerunners in Russian literature—notably Gogol, Dostoevsky, Turgenev, and Tolstoy. In addition they resurrected and claimed as their own previously neglected nineteenth-century Russian poets such as Karolina Pavlova, Fedor Tiutchev, and Afanasii Fet. As for the ideas of the movement, its aesthetics combined several French elements: the decadents' rejection of bourgeois materialism and of utilitarian literature, Baudelaire's theory of "correspondences," Verlaine's experiments with prosody and evocation of moods codified in his "Art poètique" ("De la musique avant tout choses"), and Mallarmé's awareness of the limits of language, expressed in "Les Fenêtres."

Sologub, who translated Verlaine into Russian, and whose home, along with Viacheslav Ivanov's and the Merezhkovskys', was one of the places where symbolists congregated every week for discussion and readings,[26] was well aware of these intellectual currents. In *The Petty Demon* the influence of European modernism is evident in the character of Liudmila, a decadent young woman who loves beautiful clothing, exotic perfumes and who dreams about snakes. There is also at least one allusion to Nietzsche's *The Birth of Tragedy* in one of the narrator's comments about Peredonov:[27]

> Blinded by the delusions of personality and of a separate existence, he did not understand the Dionysian, primordial ecstasies which were exultantly crying out in nature. (311)

The philosophical basis of Russian symbolism (which developed a little later than the aesthetic, in the first years of the twentieth century) came indirectly from Russian Orthodox theology via the sometimes eccentric religious writings of Vladimir Soloviev (1853-1900). Many of the symbolists admired Soloviev who was also a poet, a professor of philosophy and a religious wanderer, but it was Viacheslav Ivanov, the symbolist theoretician, who interpreted and adapted Soloviev's work. The symbolists accepted Soloviev's belief that art could reveal the hidden nature of the world and thus transfigure it, along with the corollary that "art is knowledge, not simply a vehicle of knowledge, but a mode of knowing,"[28] that is, art does not merely describe reality but is a way of knowing ultimate truths. Soloviev's influence also made itself felt in his fascination with the mystical Eastern Orthodox figure of Sophia (a female force associated with Divine Wisdom), as well as in a deeply felt need to reconcile the individualism of decadence with some form of communality through art.[29] Although, as I will show, Sologub was accused of being irreligious by several of his fellow symbolists, he was clearly attracted to the religious wing of the movement. In its early years he frequented the salon of Zinaida Gippius and her husband Dmitrii Merezhkovsky, where religious questions were discussed at length; moreover, most of *The Petty Demon* originally appeared in *Voprosi Zhizni*, the religious–philosophical journal founded by the Merezhkovskys.[30] In the novel itself one suspects that Sologub is expressing his own religious feelings when the narrator, in a rather uncharacteristic lyric and fervent digression, describes the Russian Orthodox mass as "the mystery of the transubstantiation of inert matter into a force dissolving the bonds of death" (243–244).

If the variety of sources symbolism drew on did not make defining the movement difficult enough, additional confusion arose because no two symbolists accepted the same principles. Beliefs varied, not only from one symbolist to another, but with certain symbolists from year to year. Blok, for example, in 1905 shocked his fellow-symbolists by suddenly transmogrifying the "beautiful lady" of his poetry (a figure connected with Sophia) into a prostitute. In general, overlapping, often mutually hostile, subgroups (each with its own journal) were part of symbolism from the very beginning. Indeed, it may be, as Oleg Maslenikov rather cynically suggests, that the only ideas the symbolists had in common were an anti–utilitarian orientation to literature and a desire for fame; that the movement was composed of a group of fierce individualists who only submitted themselves to a "party program" in order to advance symbolism and hence their own careers.[31]

Nevertheless, it is possible to state some very broad philosophical and aesthetic premises that were generally accepted. In the most general terms all symbolists adhered to a dualistic,

Platonic system that contrasted the "real" material, phenomenal
world with an unknown, but intuitable, higher sphere, variously
referred to as *l'azur*, the world of pure values or a transcendental
order.   In marked contrast to the neo-realists they believed in art
for art's sake.   Through symbols, they believed, the artist reveals
to the reader the existence of the eternal in the ephemeral, "the
general truth that lies hidden in the bewildering multiplicity of the
particular."[32]   This implies that art gives meaning to life and that
the role of the artist is very meaningful indeed.   Hints of these
attitudes can be seen in *The Petty Demon*, in which the only
positive character is an actor (that is, an artist) who saves Sasha
from an enraged crowd; furthermore, as Peredonov goes mad he
seems to grow increasingly aware of a second, higher realm,
inaccessible to most of mankind: "His mad, dull eyes wandered and
didn't fix on things, as though he wanted to look beyond them, to
the other side of the material world, and he was searching for
apertures of some kind" (366).

As a result of several factors the symbolists were more
conservative politically than the neo-realists.   By and large they
came from more well-to-do families (Sologub was the only
symbolist of proletarian origin).   Their worship of the Nietzschean
cult of the individual implied a detached attitude toward social
causes and society as a whole; and those who were led by
Merezhkovsky and Gippius were deeply committed to renewing the
Russian Orthodox Church, and not willing to break with this most
politically reactionary of Russian institutions.   Finally, their art
itself was unapologetically elitist, written for the cultured few who
could understand it.

I have characterized the symbolist movement as neo-romantic,
a term that needs some clarification.   J. D. West points out that
symbolism is part of modernism (long accepted as a neo-romantic
phenomenon), and that the symbolists borrowed a great deal of
their terminology and concepts from the romantics—from Goethe,
Blake, Novalis, Schopenhauer, Baudelaire, and Coleridge.   The
symbolists also shared many of the romantics' values: an exaltation
of the individual, disillusionment with society, interest in the
exotic, the alien, the historical, in fantasy and irrationality, and,
above all, a sense of the poet as mediator between mankind and
the universe.   There are, however, some significant differences
between symbolism and romanticism.   For one thing, the

symbolists were far too artistically self-conscious and in love with artifice to share the romantics' enthusiasm for nature, and far too concerned with art and the artist to idealize the common man. They were also very abstract. Their basic concept of a two-tiered reality, with only the initiated having access to the higher symbolic level, led them to erect elaborate metaphysical systems and often to intellectualize their feelings in a most unromantic way.[33]

In overview, the neo-realists and neo-romantics were two distinct streams of Russian literature that continued to diverge up to and after the 1917 Revolution. In the 1890s, however, Russian symbolism was still too new and Russian literature in much too ferment for these two tendencies even to be distinguished. Tolstoy, if one were to believe both sides, belonged to both groups. The Gorky group adapted him on the basis of his realism and anti-government activity, while the symbolists pointed to his craftsmanship and the rich use of metaphor in his earlier work. Actually Tolstoy belonged to neither. He expressed his strong disapproval of the decadents in *What Is Art?* (1898), characterizing their work as affected, unintelligible, perverted, elitist and not good art according to his views: "Good artists . . . compose works to be intelligible to all men . . . . Good art always pleases everyone . . . . Art is the transmission of feelings flowing from man's religious perception." On the other hand, Tolstoy's crusade against violence did not allow him to feel comfortable with revolutionary ideology, and the inextinguishable traces of his upper-class origins and concern for good form created distance between him and proletarian writers. Although Gorky seems to have fascinated him as a social phenomenon, Tolstoy was intolerant and patronizing of Gorky's lower-class origins and lack of literary polish.[34]

Politics made strange bedfellows. Despite vastly different styles and approaches, Chekhov, Tolstoy and Gorky were grouped together as "progressives" on the basis of their shared dissatisfactions with the Russian social order (expressed in Tolstoy's anti-government and anti-clerical activities, Gorky's proletarian heroes and political activism, and Chekhov's muted references to a better future). Friendships also made for strange politics. Initially, writers did not think in terms of literary camps or aesthetic polemics, but often grouped themselves according to personal affinities. For example, Gorky's "Revolutionary School of Fiction" included such non-revolutionaries as Bunin and Kuprin (both of whom promptly emigrated after 1917), Korolenko, who denounced the Bolshevik Revolution from Finland, and Andreev, whose often heavy-handed spiritual allegories made him a very dubious realist. Briusov, although described as the "Peter the Great of Russian Symbolism," was an early member of Gorky's *Sreda* group and later embraced the Bolshevik Revolution.[35]   So did Bely, a major symbolist writer, critic, and theoretician.

Around the turn of the century the two groups began to polarize, to develop their own separate publications and aesthetics. The unsuccessful liberal revolution of 1905 was the final divider, separating the radicals from the liberals within Gorky's *Znanie* groups and the symbolists from the revolutionaries.   The symbolists, after some morbid apocalyptic excitement during the revolution, artistically and metaphysically expressed by the "mystical anarchist" splinter group, quickly lost interest in politics and lapsed into a kind of fatalistic mood of expectancy.[36] Gorky, on the other hand, was forced to leave the country in 1905 and settled in Capri, where he worked with the Bolsheviks, leaving his most faithful followers to carry on his literary work at home.[37]

Both neo-realists and neo-romantics can be said to have lost by the split.   The Gorky group maintained its political integrity and social commitment but often sacrificed artistic integrity and craftmanship.   In socialist realism, the official and obligatory literary style of the Soviet state that was propagated with Gorky's help at the First Congress of the Union of Soviet Writers in 1934, neo-realism can be said to have been taken to its logical, utilitarian extreme.   Writers became, in Stalin's words, "engineers of the human soul," not creative artists but molders of public opinion.[38]   The symbolists also lost by the split; although they produced some wonderfully mystical and exotic works, including elegant poetry and short stories, complex essays and heady metaphysics, after the first decade of the twentieth century, they became increasingly abstract and abstruse, turning inward away from society, and thus cutting their movement off from the flow of Russian history.

The Petty Demon cannot be classified as either neo-realistic or neo-romantic though it clearly illuminates the entire literary period in which it took shape.   Sologub, having an acute political awareness lacking in other symbolists and a directness that any neo-realist might envy, describes and castigates the conditions of the '80s and '90s—the political persecution of national minorities and the official policies by which the government tried to keep Russia a stratified society. Indeed, P. A. Kogan views *The Petty Demon* largely in political terms as a spiritual political history of the times; hence he considers Peredonov, Sologub's mad protagonist, as a Russian Everyman:

> The '90s created a type previously unknown in Russian literature. The "guardianship" created it, that guardianship which with infinite wiles entangled the Russian man in the street. The man in the street, accustomed himself to the thought that he was guilty, always guilty, regardless of whether he behaved himself with total propriety, or nurtured evil designs. He could always be convicted of something . . . . Peredonov is a product of the guardians. What is characteristic of Peredonov is not his humbleness or his terror before the authorities, but the very particular form in which this humbleness and terror is manifested . . . . Peredonov's insanity is not ordinary craziness . . . . It is that objectless terror, that anxious expectation which filled Russian life, transforming it into a gray, tormented existence. Peredonov is insane but the entire atmosphere is imbued with his insanity.[39]

In addition to these seemingly neo-realistic features Kogan enumerates, one immediately recognizes that the setting of the novel—provincial Russia at the end of the nineteenth century—and the subject—the petty cruelty and nervous breakdown of a *gimnaziia* teacher—contrast with the exotic settings and heavy religious overtones of symbolist novels such as Merezhkovsky's *Christ and Anti-Christ* (1896-1904), Bely's *Silver Dove* (1909), and even Kuzmin's *Wings* (1906). Unlike Bely's *Petersburg* (a late and brilliant symbolist work with allusions to anthroposophy), there is no elaborate metaphysical system underlying events in Sologub's novel.

Yet despite elements so uncharacteristic of symbolism, Sologub's positive and mystical attitude toward religion, his intimations of a higher world, and his touches of decadence all show that he was part of the mainstream of the symbolist movement. Furthermore, as will be seen, the novel's peculiar structure and hallucinatory atmosphere are far from realistic.

I have suggested that the mixture of neo-realistic and

symbolist elements in *The Petty Demon* reflect the fact that Sologub wrote the novel between 1892 and 1902, at a time when the two trends were not yet polarized, when *The Northern Herald* was still featuring works by Chekhov, Tolstoy and Gorky side by side with symbolist poetry and translations of Ibsen, Maeterlinck and D'Annunzio, while symbolism was still attempting to define and separate itself from other literary currents.[40]   The novel's unique position in literary history may partly account for its stormy reception among conservative critics, which will be discussed in the next chapter.   At the same time, its very strangeness exerts a powerful effect on readers that makes it impossible to dismiss. Praising Sologub's originality, Aleksandr Blok in 1907 described *The Petty Demon* as "one of the most outstanding things in Russian literature in recent years," and Dmitrii Mirsky twenty years later called it "the most perfect novel since the death of Dostoevsky."[41] Time, and the novel's continued popularity, have confirmed their judgments.

Chapter 2
Reception

The critical furor that greeted the first complete edition of *The Petty Demon* was intensified, perhaps by the novel's delayed publication.[1] By 1907 symbolism was in full flower and Sologub was considered an established member of this still controversial movement. Thus doctrinaire symbolists and anti-symbolists often treated the novel as a product of the movement in its current form, superimposing on it the literary polemics of the moment.[2] Nor, as we will see, did either side hesitate to attack Sologub personally in order to make a point. In addition, the liberal 1905 revolution had come and gone, leaving political opinions polarized. Some "left" critics in the tradition of Belinsky and Dobroliubov used reviews of *The Petty Demon* to comment on the political scene; ignoring the decadent and symbolist aspects of the novel, they praised *The Petty Demon* as a realistic depiction of political oppression in Russia.[3] (Sologub quickly fell out of favor with the political left when the first part of his blatantly unrealistic trilogy appeared later in 1907.)[4] Solugub's deliberately irritating public persona also contributed to the intense critical reaction; several reviewers responded by treating *The Petty Demon* (along with the rest of Sologub's poetry, plays and prose) as case material to illustrate what they considered to be his character pathology.[5] But underlying all of the controversy was the strangeness and stature of the novel itself. While generally recognizing the novel as a major work of literature, most critics, for reasons I will consider, had difficulty addressing it in its own terms and concentrated instead on extrinsic elements. Nevertheless, this criticism illuminates the novel both directly by what it says and indirectly by the aspects of the novel it ignores.

The most interesting criticism was written by Sologub's fellow symbolists. Although many of these articles say more about them than about Sologub, as though he were merely the pretext they used to set out their own ideas, two essays by Aleksandr Blok from 1907 stand out as being unusually sensitive and objective.

The first, "O realistakh" ("Concerning Realists"), appeared in
Zolotoe runo (*The Golden Fleece*) and treated Sologub along with
such neo-realists as Gorky, Serefimich, Andreev, and others of the
Znanie group.   That Blok saw the appropriateness of discussing
Sologub in a realistic context is in itself an unusual perception.   In
the section devoted to *The Petty Demon* Blok disagrees with one of
the many reviewers who tried to identify Sologub with his
unpleasant protagonist and argues that the question is not that
simple: "Peredonov is *each of us*, or if you like, I will say it more
gently: in each of us there exists Peredonovism" (italics Blok's).
In a more controversial passage Blok defends the novel against
charges of obscenity by insisting on the purity of Sasha's dalliance
with Liudmila:

> The episode of innocent lovers' play actually can be
> read separately and reread like poetry . . . . Liudmila's
> room is on the second floor, and there these ethereal
> petty bourgeois, these heavenly philistines, celebrate
> their beauty.   The only pity is that their fragrant flesh
> can live in harmony with such small spirit.   But this
> erotica is nothing terrible.   Here everything is pure,
> fragrant, and unashamed of the sun's rays.[6]

Subsequent critics disagreed with Blok about the nature of the
Sasha-Liudmila subplot, and as I will discuss in Chapter 3, I, too,
believe that this episode does not offer any relief from Peredonov's
destructiveness and pettiness, but merely presents Peredonovism in
another form.

Blok's second essay, which appeared in *Pereval* (*The Passage*),
discussed not only *The Petty Demon* but also Sologub's earlier
novel, *Tiazhelye Sny (Bad Dreams)*, and some of his short stories
from a symbolist point of view.   After considering Sologub's
natural, unstilted language and his use of epic and Gogolian styles,
Blok linked Sologub's distinctive prose to the symbolist aesthetic:

> But the clue to the originality of Sologub's work is not
> only in the language.   Rather, it has its roots in his
> favorite device; this device, which is always fresh despite
> repetition, consists of the following: in reading simple,
> realistic scenes you begin to feel little by little that the
> writer is preparing himself for something—as if
> everything we just read was observed through a
> transparent curtain which softened features that were

too harsh. But now the author raises the curtain and reveals to us, always for a short time, the monstrousness of life. The task is to show the reader something monstrously absurd in such a way that it can be examined without interference, like an animal in a cage. This animal is human mediocrity, and the cage is the device of stylization and symmetry. In symmetrical and stylized forms we observe something which in itself is hideous and formless. That is why it howls at us in an otherworldly and unreal way—and beyond it we see non-existence, a diabolical countenance, the chaos of hell. But this is only the highest reality disclosed, a moment which flares up and imprints itself clearer than anything else on the memory, just as in life we remember those wild burning minutes, whether good or evil, which made one's head spin and ache.[7]

Although in this passage Blok may be reading the later sophistication of symbolist philosophy into Sologub's early work, in general he was one of the few symbolists who was equally aware of Sologub's neo-realistic and symbolist aspects.

By contrast, Zinaida Gippius (who, with Dmitrii Merezhkovsky, founded the religious wing of symbolism), wrote in quite a different vein. Her article, "Slezinka Peredonova," ("Peredonov's Little Tear,") which appeared in November 1908 in *Rech' (Speech)* is elegantly and even brilliantly written, but it says far more about her religious concerns than it does about the novel. Furthermore, her digs at Sologub and her tone of spiritual one-upmanship leave a somewhat unpleasant impression. The article is subtitled "What F. Sologub Doesn't Know," and it starts with a short excerpt from a poem Gippius dedicated to him, in which she contrasted his apparent knowledge of religious mysteries with what she considered his actual spiritual shallowness. She wrote, "The wise man and prophet extracted water, living water, from the well, but did not see the truth itself."[8] She then insisted that despite Sologub's statements to the contrary (in his preface to the second edition of the novel), Peredonov is a self-portrait. From this she argued that Sologub felt uncomfortable because his repulsive anti-hero resembled him so closely, and that he therefore was unable to understand, defend, or even examine Peredonov.[9] Nonetheless, Gippius continued, by the end of the novel, she found herself feeling sorry for Peredonov, even though she knew he deserved to suffer.   And, according to her, this involuntary sympathy for the character is the novel's true value.   Peredonov's richly deserved suffering, she wrote, was a "super-injustice" compared to the ordinary injustice experienced by innocent victims; they, at least, have everyone's sympathy, but no one—not even Sologub, she claimed—feels sorry for Peredonov.   "He is ugly, spiteful, dirty and dull, he is nothing, an absolute nonentity; however he is created, he exists, he is an 'I.' "   Gippius' argument amounted to an embellishment of Ivan's speech in *The Brothers Karamazov* in which he rejected God's world in the name of innocent children who suffer.   But while Ivan's speech was a genuine cry of incomprehension and anguish, Gippius, in demanding that God and/or Sologub account for Peredonov, implied that mankind (that is, people who shared her views), were morally superior to both:

> There are many tortured children, many who suffer
> innocently and not innocently . . . but there are even
> more Peredonovs, hopelessly suffering, beggars in every
> sense and cursed by all.   We know this, except we
> rarely think about it.   But when we do, when we see
> and feel, we stop disdaining the Peredonovs, we protect
> them, and in protecting them, ask, "How didst Thou,
> who created Peredonov, dare to create him?   How wilt
> Thou answer for him?   Tell us, we need to know."

Although Gippius correctly perceived Peredonov's underlying pathos, her criticism, it seems to me, fails on two counts.   First, she credited herself with having discovered that it is possible to sympathize with Peredonov and implied that the novel had to be filtered through her finer sensibilities before its significance could become clear.   It seems more likely, however, that we feel sorry for Peredonov at the end not in spite of Sologub, but because of him, that it was his power as a writer that enabled him to create a repulsive yet genuinely pathetic character whom we cannot easily dismiss.   In subsequent chapters I will demonstrate that this, indeed, is the case.

On a more basic level, Gippius' entire method of analysis is open to question.   She discusses the novel as if its only value lay in the fact that it illustrated her pet ideas—Sologub's supposed lack of religious enlightenment, Dostoevsky's religious views, the problem of evil in the world—instead of examining *The Petty*

Demon in its own terms. Her approach, as we will see, is typical of many of Sologub's fellow-symbolists who, with the narcissism characteristic of their movement, often used their reviews of Sologub's work as self-advertisements.

Another symbolist with a strong interest in religion was Viacheslav Ivanov. But unlike Gippius, who was interested in revitalizing the Russian Orthodox Church, Ivanov wished to reconcile Christianity and paganism by putting the Elysian mysteries into a Christian context and by interpreting Dionysus as a forerunner of Christ. Ivanov's concerns were not particularly unusual for his times. Due, perhaps, to discoveries in the newly developing discipline of anthropology, there was a general interest in the interconnection of mysticism, mythology, and religion as witnessed by the works of Nietzsche, Wagner, and later James Frazer. Sologub would seem to have had a great deal of sympathy with Ivanov's views. When the first installment (January, 1904) of Ivanov's series of lectures, "The Hellenic Religion of the Suffering God," began to appear in *Novyi put'* (*The New Path*), they were accompanied by seven Sologub poems entitled "Hymns of the Suffering Dionysus." But despite the similarity of their beliefs, language and imagery, which will be discussed in more detail below, Ivanov used a 1904 review of a collection of Sologub short stories to emphasize their differences. Ivanov's writing is somewhat abstruse, but his essay is worth considering for what it indicates about his attitude toward Sologub, and by extension, *The Petty Demon.*

Ivanov believed that because Sologub's world view is not anchored in Christianity (an assumption which, as we have seen, is open to question), its mythology degenerates into satanism.

> The mythological world view [he wrote] may or may not be religious. In the latter case it becomes purely demonic. Such is the atmosphere which is summoned up the work of F. Sologub and is breathed by strange souls, wanderers passing through the world with the seal of the other world on their brow.[10]

He described Sologub's god as a "blind, yet staring pantheon . . . a faceless, thousand-eyed choir of supernatural beings" and contrasted this with his own Christian-based mythology, which he explained through the following analogy. Just as white light separates into colors when passed through a prism, so God remains one but allows Himself to be manifested in all the phenomena of the world ("refracted in rainbows of existence"). God, Ivanov felt, enjoys this manifestation and thus wills the illusion of diversity to continue, for when everything is reunited again into white light, the universe will cease to exist. Sologub, however, he believed, had excluded himself from this joyful vision of life. "Apparently the artist does not believe it is possible to 'turn and become as little children,' and not believing in this mystical renaissance, he does not see the possibility of a purified life, of a single correct answer to life."

Despite the differences in style, Ivanov's review has a great deal in common with Gippius'. Both praised Sologub's work while citing it as an indication that something was seriously wrong with its author; both used the review as an opportunity to present some of their own ideas as superior to Sologub's; both perceived Sologub (incorrectly, I believe) as areligious, someone who created his own hell instead of embracing God's world. As we will see, many other critics also expressed grave concern for Sologub's spiritual well-being, an unusual critical stance that probably reflected discomfort with Sologub's work and was a way of putting as much distance as possible between Sologub and themselves. In Ivanov's case the discomfort with Sologub must have been even greater, given the similarity of many of their ideas. It is also possible that Sologub in some way provoked condescending reactions, a point that will be discussed later in this chapter.

Of all the criticism written by fellow symbolists, Andrei Bely's two articles were probably the most subjective and ambivalent, although certainly among the most interesting. In a 1907 review of a collection of Sologub's short stories Bely praised him highly, calling him "one of the foremost stylists of our time."[11] Bely also praised Sologub's vision, describing him as a purely Russian writer, but one who according to him was in touch with what he called the "Buddhist" characteristics of Russia's land and people. This term requires some explanation. In contrast to the optimistic, self-determined energy of the West, Buddhism for Bely seems to have had negative connotations, representing what he considered to be the empty, passive, death-embracing Eastern aspect of the Russian temperament, the unmoving and unmoved lethargy of the provinces. "There is something Buddhist in the Russian landscape," Bely wrote. "The bared teeth of ravines and the sadly waving fields—does this not all speak of Nirvana? In the Russian landscape Sologub can discern the austerity of Buddhism and in the sleepy philistine, a representative of the stupified blockhead, Buddha." Sologub, he believed, depicted the "eternal dream" of provincial Russians, which is a kind of death. Bely ended the article by calling the collection possibly Sologub's "best book" and wrote in conclusion, "It is a sure sign that the writer is growing, his talent becoming more subtle and steady. Indeed, we expect from him new creative incarnations, new words poisoned by death."

In this article Bely found Sologub's elegant style and somewhat morbid vision very appropriate to his subject, the deadness of provincial Russia. Sologub, he wrote, had discovered and described the essential Buddhist nature of Russia and was continuing to grow as an artist. One can hardly imagine a more positive review.

In 1908, however, in one of the abrupt turn-abouts the symbolists were famous for, Bely wrote an article entitled "Dalai-lama iz Sapozhka" ("The Dali Lama from Sapozhok") which, according to V. F. Khodasevich, Sologub still held against Bely fifteen years later.[12] It is not difficult to see why Sologub was so angry: in a triumph of reductive criticism, Bely diminished *The Petty Demon*, along with a play by Sologub and a collection of his short stories, to an unvarying dialectical formula. He went so far as to provide a two-page chart with quotations from various Sologub works grouped under the headings of "nature," "unconscious," and "conscious," each of which was divided into thesis, antithesis, and synthesis. In effect, Bely was trying to demonstrate that if you've read one Sologub work you've read them all.

As though this were not enough, Bely then compared Sologub to a cheap magician who addresses himself to children and tries to scare them with fraudulent tricks. After one grows up, or catches on, Bely implies, the tricks are not so impressive.

> Oh, you hocus-pocus-er! The magician pocuses, puts on an Armenian robe, and waves around two little bottles. 'Here, children, I have these two little bottles. Guzzle one and you will become immortal . . . guzzle the other and . . . before you deadly non-existence will appear.' Examine the Armenian; he intimidates, he manufactures a boogy man from his robe.
> Don't believe it, children; our kind hocus-pocus-er is

Fedor Kuz'mich Sologub. What a comfort, children, it
is for us to read him! You will grow up and read him,
you will read him and understand him . . . [13]

At the end of the article, instead of praising Sologub for his
evocation of the Buddhist nature of Russia, as he had a year
earlier, Bely reproved Sologub for "hole worshipping" and compared
him to a holy fool (*iurodivyi*) who long ago made his point and
who is beginning to bore people:

> Buddhism is fine in Tibet: In Sapozhok [a provincial
> Russian town Bely uses to designate the settings of all
> Sologub's works] it amounts only to hole worshipping.
> He sits in a hut and there is a hole in the hut and he
> prays into the hole, "O hut of mine, o hole of mine,
> save me." But his great holy foolishness painfully
> exposes us. After all, we are hole worshippers, too,
> only secret ones. Our secret became obvious in
> Sologub. He just sat himself down in a corner as he
> was—in a frockcoat, with a glass of tea—he sat and
> exposed us. And exposed by him, we must tell him,
> "What we have to say to you is—Get up!"

> Squatting in a corner before one's own shadow is
> holy foolishness, that is, a knightly deed: in Western
> Europe long ago there were knights inspiring respect; in
> Sapozhok long ago there were holy fools inspiring
> superstitious terror. Sologub's sitting before an empty
> corner inspires terror as well: Enough, we are not
> children. Let us approach this tremendous artist and
> say to him, "Thank you, man of God; with your staff
> you showed us our blind death, and we saw that we
> have no blind death."

Bely temporized at the end by calling Sologub a "tremendous
artist" and by giving him credit for having pointed out the empty
Buddhist quality of the Russian temperament—something that
must be faced so that it can be overcome. However, the
impression that remains after reading this article is that Bely
considered Sologub's art to be fraudulent and easily outgrown.
Furthermore, the apparent ease with which Bely praised and then
attacked Sologub in these two articles, using similar terms, leads
one to suspect that Bely, not Sologub, is the subject of these

essays—that Sologub merely supplies the theme for a *jeu d'esprit.*[14]

In Bely's article we see the combination of annoyance and wit that characterizes most of the criticism written by Sologub's fellow symbolists; if these articles do not address *The Petty Demon* directly, at least they reflect the individual and interesting views of the authors. In turning to the reviews written by lesser critics, one is quickly struck by their repetitiveness. Article after article describes Sologub in the same terms—"solipsistic," "decadent," "morbid," or "anti-life"—in a tone of fascination if the reviewer supports symbolism, or abhorrence if he disapproves of it; again and again one reads that Peredonov is really Sologub's self-portrait. I do not wish to suggest that these reviews are uniformly bad; indeed, they contain many valuable insights about Sologub's literary progenitors, the evolution of protagonists in his works, the relationship between his poetry and prose, and the interplay between realism and symbolism in *The Petty Demon* itself. Furthermore, one can understand the critics' emphasis on the underside of Sologub's psyche since the first part of his trilogy, a darker and not entirely successful work (which I will discuss further in Chapter 9), also came out in 1907, probably affecting the evaluation of *The Petty Demon.* Nonetheless, in reading these reviews one feels that the critics generally did not respond freshly and openly to *The Petty Demon* as a novel; rather, they took as their text the current mythology about Sologub the man, or the body of previous Sologub criticism. Before asking why, it is worth looking at the most common critical cliches about Sologub and what lay behind them.

The various elements in the Sologub myth did have some factual basis; in particular, the often repeated charge that he was a solipsist should be examined in some detail.[15] Sologub did write several works in different genres that could be understood as assertions that no one else existed in the universe besides himself.[16] One article considered particularly outrageous was called " 'Ia,' Kniga sovershennogo samoutverzhdeniia" (" 'I': The Book of Complete Self-Affirmation"); it was described by one critic as Sologub's "self-deification."[17] The word "book" in the title of this poetic essay appears to refer to a book of the Bible; the essay itself is only four pages long. Contrary to Russian usage, the first person pronoun is capitalized throughout. The essay started by maintaining "I and I alone exist," and ended by calling the Father, Son and Holy Spirit "my latest idols"—sentiments which, if taken literally, would certainly have upset devout people of many religions. (Sologub, it should be mentioned, was not at all averse to shocking people.) In this and similar essays, however, I believe that Sologub was restating, in only slightly different form, ideas that had appeared in Nietzsche's *Birth of Tragedy from the Spirit of Music* (1872) regarding the cult of Dionysus, as well as those in the work of Viacheslav Ivanov, mentioned above. Problems arose because Sologub, unlike Ivanov, wrote from the point of view of the spirit of the universe. In the hymns accompanying the above-mentioned Ivanov article, for example, Sologub did not write about the sufferings of Dionysus but as if he were the suffering Dionysus. While Ivanov made it clear that his mythology was to be understood in a Christian context, Sologub did not, and it was therefore possible to misinterpret Sologub's "I" as standing for not a divine principle but himself. It is also possible that Sologub did not take these writings very seriously; after all, he did not include them in the twenty volumes of his *Collected Works*. There is, however, a clear continuity between these essays and some of his important, and very serious, aesthetic works. In "Elisaveta" and "The Theater of One Will," for example, the work of art, or the artist, becomes the center of an artistic universe and, like the speaker in the solipsistic essays, assumes a multitude of transient "guises" or masks. Many critics who called Sologub a "solipsist" apparently did not examine these writings carefully in the context of the rest of his work.

A second element of the Sologub myth—that he had a peculiar sense of humor—also had a factual basis. It seems clear from many memoirs about him that Sologub went out of his way to intimidate younger writers and to maintain a dour school teacher's facade. Il'ia Erenburg described Sologub in his memoirs as "more a headmaster than a poet" and several contemporaries describe their first meeting with him as an unpleasant and even frightening experience. Georgii Chulkov wrote of how Sologub embarrassed him when they were first introduced in 1906 by making fun of the title of his article, "The Distances are Brightening," which had just been published in *Vesy*. "Sologub having heard my last name and shaking my hand, said slyly screwing up his eyes, 'But I think they're darkening.' . . . In my inexperience I didn't know how to react to my honorable interlocutor's irony." Konstantin Fedin recalls his first impression of Sologub's "papery dry face with bilious coils of two motionless creases at the corners of the mouth and the glassy sobriety of light gray eyes. The glimmer of his narrow eyeglasses corresponded with his entire face, strengthening the coldness of his eyes and the arrogant mockery and bitter outline of his lips . . . . He liked to drive his interlocutor into a corner, to inspire embarrassment and awkwardness. He would play with unresourceful or bashful people like a cat with a mouse." One critic refers to a legend that Sologub was never seen to laugh in his life. All the same, it is difficult to excuse the reviewer who, missing the deadpan humor of *The Petty Demon* entirely, claimed that Sologub had not intentionally written a funny book but was just describing the world as he saw it. Calling Sologub a satirist *malgré lui*, the critic self-importantly proposed to "restore the author's rights, showing that his assigned role as a satirist is a total injustice."[18]

Perhaps because of Sologub's irritating yet inaccessible public persona many critics analyzed his work in order to find the key to the "real" (and to their minds psychologically unstable) Sologub. Such attempts at diagnosing Sologub's purported psychological problems constituted the most popular critical cliché of all. A strong element of hostility is evident in much of this writing in which critics identified Sologub with Peredonov, speculated with relish about his personal problems and characterized his work as decadent, morbid, demonic or even insane. Indeed, several suggested that Sologub needed a psychiatrist.[19] Similarly, Evgenii Lundberg described Sologub as "impotent in the face of passion, afraid of all fulfillment and embodiment" and claimed that all his work expressed one sentiment: *"I am not with you, I am beyond the pale"* (italics his). And A. Dolinin, who described Sologub as frightened by the world and full of "Peredonovian fears," gleefully went on to picture him as a blind and humiliated slave, screaming and beating himself against a locked door that barred him from the secret of life.[20]

The pervasive note of irritation and even anger in most of these reviews—symbolist and nonsymbolist alike—suggests that Sologub was a very annoying man and *The Petty Demon* a very provocative novel. In fact, Sologub encouraged the hostile furor that surrounded his novel by baiting his critics. He deliberately remained an enigma by using his pseudonym, Sologub (his last name was Teternikov), in private as well as in public life, and by withholding almost all biographical information about himself until 1914.[21] Furthermore, he used his introductions to the various

editions of *The Petty Demon* to insult his readers, and, in
particular, his critics.   In the second edition he insisted that the
petty world of the novel was a mirror of the reader's world; in the
fifth, that Peredonov, the novel's crude anti-hero, had become a
literary critic, and in the introduction to the seventh, he compared
his soul to a Parisienne in fancy dress and light sandals and his
critics to a crude man in a peasant blouse and greased boots who
steps on her foot.   These jibes must have irritated the critics and
made it even harder to discuss his work objectively, and thus the
novel rarely received the calm attention it deserved.   In all the
controversy about Sologub it must have difficult for critics to
acknowledge the novel's power, and even those few critics who
admitted that the novel made them feel uncomfortable did not
consider why it affected them so strongly.[22]

But why did so many critics write about their own brand of
symbolism   or   analyze   Sologub's   personality—often   many
times[23]—and with such irritation?   Why did so few critics analyze
the novel itself, its peculiarity, its composition, its effect?   How is
it that the critics never even asked themselves why they were
annoyed?   It was not merely because Sologub's irritating manner
made them unwilling to reveal their feelings.   Blok was right in
saying that critics attacked Peredonovism in Sologub in order not
to see it in themselves, but I believe that the entire answer is
more complicated.   I think that *The Petty Demon* is formally
unique, unlike any novel written before or after it, both in its
structure and in its effect on the reader.   It violated the critics'
expectations of what a novel should be, and it made them feel
very uncomfortable.   Not wanting to examine the disturbing,
unpleasant feelings the novel raised, and lacking the kind of
rigorous, post-structuralist literary analysis which would have made
such an examination possible, they rather vented their irritation in
direct or oblique attacks on Sologub.   Yet the very volume of
these attacks is a tribute to the novel's artistry and power since
critics would not have reacted so violently to a mediocre work.

In later chapters I will examine in detail both the novel's
peculiar structure and its strange effect on the reader, showing how
the two are related.   As a basis for that discussion, however, I will
first briefly digress and consider the unusual place of *The Petty
Demon* in the evolution of the novel as a genre, both in Russia
and in Europe.

Chapter 3
The Petty Demon and the Novel Genre

For the twenty-two years preceding Sologub's completion of *The Petty Demon* no outstanding Russian novel had appeared; nor, as we have seen, was there much interest in the genre, since both the neo-realists and the symbolists preferred to express themselves in short stories, critical essays, novellas, poetry and plays. I believe that much of the power and uniqueness of *The Petty Demon* is due to the fact that since the realistic Russian novel of the '60s and '70s was far too old-fashioned to accommodate a modernistic sensibility, in writing *The Petty Demon* Sologub was forced to redesign the genre for his own purposes. This feat was all the more remarkable because he did so single-handedly.

In the West a community of writers—Conrad, James, Proust, Joyce and others—continued to experiment with the novel throughout the late nineteenth and early twentieth centuries, expanding it in theme and structure to suit their purposes, but no such community or continuity of genre existed in Russia. On the other hand, because each symbolist (starting with Sologub) had to redesign the genre for himself, the best novels to come out of the symbolist movement (such as *The Petty Demon*, Kuzmin's *Wings* or Bely's *Petersburg*) are startling and successful experiments, unexcelled even by the imaginative Russian novels of the 1920s.

To understand the extent of Sologub's formal originality in *The Petty Demon*, it will be necessary to consider three questions: What was the nature of the realistic novel? How was it modified and adapted to modernism in Europe at the end of the nineteenth century? And how, in contrast, did Sologub modify the genre in *The Petty Demon*?

It is not my purpose to describe and define in depth the realistic novel as a genre. Such an undertaking would be extremely difficult because, as many critics have pointed out, the novel itself has no definable poetics. Indeed, Douglas Hewitt has even questioned if we can talk about "the novel" as a genre any more than "the poem" or "the play."[1] As for the realistic novel, not only is there no accepted definition, but critics seem very reluctant to use this subgenre in the classification of novels. *Moby Dick*, for example, which certainly has realistic elements, has been variously called a "dramatic," "symbolist," and "compensatory" novel, and *Vanity Fair*, certainly in the mainstream of nineteenth-century realistic novels, has been classified as a "novel of character."[2] In general, critics invent individual and sometimes idiosyncratic systems for analyzing small numbers of novels—systems of limited applicability for any other novel. The problem is that each novel when looked at in detail turns out to be unique, and so it is difficult to generalize meaningfully about them, or, as D. H. Lawrence wrote, "All rules of construction hold good only for novels that are copies of other novels." In this case, however, I will deliberately use the broad category of the realistic novel in order to arrive at characteristics common to most nineteenth-century novels. My purpose is to establish a background of novelistic practices which can be loosely characterized as realistic and against which Sologub's originality may be more clearly understood. For this reason I will broadly define the realistic novel as ranging in time from the work of Balzac to that of Tolstoy and will use examples of some of the best-known nineteenth-century novels to test and illustrate some generalizations about the subgenre.

The second difficulty in defining realistic novels lies within the nature of realism itself. In appearing to present life as it is lived, in centering around such "real life" events as birth, marriage and death, the realistic novel uses art to create an illusion of life and thus minimizes itself as a genre. In effect, one of its conventions is the absence of conventions. If, however, we consider the realistic novel in terms of its most basic constituents: character, plot, setting and narration—categories which are broad enough to be common to all novels—a seemingly obvious but very useful principle emerges: in realistic novels, characters and what happens to them (plot) are considered foreground, the subject of the novel and the focus of interest; in contrast, narration (the way the author chooses to tell the story) and setting (the description of time and place), however important to our sense of the novel, are background aspects.[3] The author's ability to stay in the background while inducing the reader to sympathize and partially identify with the central characters accounts for the realistic focus on characters and what happens to them (plot). In *The Red and the Black*, for example, it is Julien and his fate that rivet our attention, not the particular location of events or the subtleness of Stendhal's narrative technique.

This principle has aesthetic and philosophical significance as well. Character and plot are central to realistic novels because the attention of writer and reader is on the relationship between the characters and their world as it actually is, not as it might be. In J. P. Stern's words, "Realism does not ask whether the world is real."[4] Instead, characters' destinies are worked out concretely—in the material world and in society. This destiny, consisting of birth, marriage, death, social position, wealth and poverty, is central to the realistic novel because it not only comprises the area of the characters' existence, but also constitutes the very meaning of their lives. In *Middlemarch*, for example, Dorothea's marriage to Ladislaw is vindicated by the fact that she gives birth to a son and that he is elected to Parliament. In *Great Expectations* Pip's role as hero is confirmed by the fact that he rises to a higher social class. Ontology, or ways of looking at the world, is not at issue, nor are speculations on time and space. Hence narration and setting play a secondary role.

It follows from this concern with the world as it is that in realism a very high value is placed on the protagonist's coming to terms with life. The theme of many realistic novels is *"illusions perdues"*—they recount a character's misapprehensions and show the often painful but necessary process of learning to know the world and themselves. Pip in *Great Expectations* must find out and accept the fact that his benefactor is a criminal; Raskol'nikov in *Crime and Punishment* must realize that he is not a Napoleonic type; Dorothea in *Middlemarch* must see the falsity of her previous self-abnegation; Arkady in *Fathers and Sons* must become aware of the painful consequences of nihilism. Each character who goes through this process of becoming reconciled with reality is rewarded with some understanding of the pattern of his or her life and sense of inner peace. As Maurice Shroder writes: "The novel records the passage from a state of innocence to a state of experience, from that of ignorance which is bliss to a mature recognition of the actual way of the world."[5]

This emphasis on coming to terms with the material world in no way means that the mental or spiritual dimension of life is excluded in realism. On the contrary, the spirit is also considered part of the world and is never questioned. The meditations,

meditations, thoughts, and feelings of characters such as Levin and Karenina in *Anna Karenina*, for example, are just as important as their actions, and in fact give those actions meaning. "Realism depends upon a balance between mind and world, inner and outer, set in a certain point in time," Stern writes. "It is this balance of inner making and outward matching which creates the fiction of a shared reality."[6]   That is, the author gives equal weight to the physical and nonphysical aspects of characters and situations, and thus creates, out of the world he shares with the reader, a new world which the reader can also share.

At the end of the nineteenth century, however, the assumption that there existed a common reality began to be questioned, as was the possibility of creating a shared reality through art.   Alvin Seltzer characterized this modernist revolution in thought as a "psychological-philosophical shift from a world-view asserting ultimate order to one mandating chaos to be the deepest level of reality."[7]   This change in world view reflected a growing sense of the relativity of truth, perhaps the result of the cumulative assaults of Darwin, Bergson, Freud, and later of Einstein on the more limited but secure nineteenth-century world view.   People began to perceive themselves as irrevocably isolated from others for if, indeed, truth is relative, then everyone's truth is different and incommunicable.[8]

In art the realistic "balance between mind and world, inner and outer set in a certain point in time"[9] was disrupted and changes, expressing the new world view, began to occur in European novels.   Characters, generally transparent in realistic novels, became less knowable in Conrad, for example,[10] and plots, which in realistic novels often emulated the objectivity and structure of classical drama, in Proust and others began to resemble externalizations of thought.   Narrators, too, who had been so confidently omniscient in Tolstoy, Balzac, and Dickens, took on a limited and self-conscious quality in the novels of Henry James and his followers, while setting, the specific time and place of events, grew less concrete and more fluid in novels such as Joyce's *Ulysses* and others.

In *The Petty Demon* Sologub, like Western novelists, also rejected the realistic aesthetic as being too narrow.   Character and plot can hardly be considered the primary focus of interest; the petty cruelty and lack of a spiritual dimension in the characters makes it impossible to sympathize, much less identify, with them.

And while a great deal happens in the plot, events do not unfold in the dramatic Aristotelian manner characteristic of realistic novels: introduction, first development, turning point, second development, climax and, finally, resolution. Rather, they seem to occur arbitrarily so that the plot has a cumulative rather than an organic quality. The novel, at least on first reading, consists of a tremendous and confusing number of encounters among characters—at card parties, billiard parlors, official, unofficial and informal visits—none of which seem to develop the story or provide insight into the repulsive, caricature-like characters. Certainly, in this grotesque world there is no "shared reality" between author and reader.

Sologub uses other means to keep us interested. He charms us with humor, fascinates us with the actions of the characters, and increasingly pulls us into Peredonov's disintegrating world. Most importantly, if we make the effort to understand and experience the world he has created, he rewards that effort by meeting us halfway. In the end we discover to our surprise that there is some common ground between us and Sologub. We share his mixed feelings toward Peredonov and we experience his vision of incipient madness. This discovery of common ground with the author, where at first there seemed to be none, is a very effective device that keeps us from being overwhelmed by Peredonov's insanity. In effect, we are consoled and compensated for Peredonov's destruction by a relationship—albeit a tenuous one—with the author.

In *The Petty Demon* Sologub modified the realistic novel in a unique way. Instead of expanding the constituents of the novel (as his European counterparts did), Sologub inverted them. That is, he made setting and narration primary in his novel, and character and plot secondary. The effect of this reversal is profound and unsettling but also very powerful. Repelled by the two-dimensional, puppet-like characters and disoriented by the non-Aristotelian, additive plot, we cannot escape into unthinking identification with the characters and the movement of events. Instead, our attention is constantly forced to the surface of the novel where there is only a narrator and behind him an author juxtaposing words and ideas. Sologub, however, does not only flatten characters and plot. As I will show in the following chapters he also heightens narration and setting, which take on an almost overwhelming quality and make us feel that we, too, are being drawn into the vortrex of insanity.

One can appreciate the extent of Sologub's originality and artistry in *The Petty Demon* by comparing it with his first and much less successful novel, *Tiazhelye sny (Bad Dreams)*, the first installment of which appeared in the *Northern Herald* in July, 1895. Superficially the two novels have a great deal in common. Both are set in a small town at the end of the nineteenth century; both have protagonists who are *gimnaziia* teachers with sadistic tendencies, men who suffer from hallucinations, who cannot decide which of the local women to marry, and who ultimately commit murder. In both novels there is a sympathetic actor, a Marshal of the Nobility, and a lot of local gossip and false rumors. In *Bad Dreams*, however, Sologub was trying to write a conventional realistic novel and this prevented him from getting the necessary distance from his hero-murderer. Sologub presented Login with great seriousness as a realistic protagonist, and a spiritual descendant of Stavrogin, the tormented, misunderstood hero of Dostoevsky's *The Possessed*; there is even an ominous meeting with a tramp on a bridge. This treatment, however, does not accord with Login's affectedly decadent utterances and attitudes ("It's tiresome . . . living is tiresome"; "Tell me, what color does life seem to you, and how does it taste?"; "I have no guiding light . . . And my desires are strange"; "His heart was cold and no delusion of life had any power over it . . . . Cold and depraved was his heart"[11]). Login merely seems ludicrous. The plot is as awkward as the characters: in a forced and distasteful "happy" ending Login confesses the murder to Anna, an embodiment of purity with strong masochistic urges whom he alternately venerates and wishes to destroy. Undismayed, she tells him that he has killed the past and that they will start a new life together. The two, we are told, live happily ever after, a denouement that is both psychologically and artistically jarring.

In *The Petty Demon*, however, Sologub was able to free himself from realistic strictures. Thus he created a novel in which the theme and all the constituents work together, and so impressively that the reader experiences in modified form Peredonov's descent into madness. Sologub manages to involve us as deeply in his unconventional and repelling world as the greatest realistic novelists, while exciting in the reader a strange combination of tremendous irritation at the novel's peculiarity and a deeper satisfaction at the perfection of its execution. This, I believe, is what provoked Sologub's contemporaries to write strange reviews that combined personal attacks on him with praise of his novel.

In the following chapters I will examine Sologub's unusual reworking of the constituents of the realistic novel and attempt both to analyze its effects on Sologub's contemporaries and also understand why, in a time when we no longer expect realism, *The Petty Demon* still has such an upsetting and powerful effect. This structural approach, while important in itself, will also provide a framework within which to define the less easily categorized factors of the novel that move us.

Chapter 4
Character

Characters are not people, as E. M. Forster found it necessary to point out as late as 1927 in his *Aspects of the Novel*; bodily functions such as eating and sleeping are a far smaller part of their lives than of ours, while relationships and love are a constant preoccupation. Furthermore, should the author choose, their inner lives are completely open to our inspection. "They are not real because they are like ourselves (though they may be like us)," Forster writes, "but because they are convincing."[1] We lose sight of this distinction because the illusion that characters are living people is one of the most important conventions of the realistic novel. If the hero's changing view of the world is to have any significance, we must believe in him; if the author is to create a reality in which we can share, we must recognize and identify with the characters who experience that reality. In addition to seeming lifelike, a character must also seem to have the ability to exercise free will and to develop. Raskol'nikov's struggle in *Crime and Punishment*, for example, would have no meaning if we did not believe him to be free at any moment to confess, or not, or to commit suicide.

In examining the characters in *The Petty Demon* one becomes aware of these realistic conventions by their absence. Sologub does not attempt to create the illusion that the characters are like us, or are even lifelike. Feelings and ideals are almost completely lacking from their inner lives and rather than being preoccupied by relationships, they hardly relate to each other at all. One often comes upon bizarre, puppet-like conversations such as the following between Peredonov and Varvara:

> "I want to spit on you," Peredonov said calmly.
> "You wouldn't," cried Varvara.
> "Oh yes I would," said Peredonov.
> He stood up and, with a dull and indifferent air, spat in her face.
> "Pig," said Varvara rather calmly as if the spit had

refreshed her, and she began to wipe herself off with a napkin. (20)

The words indicate that Varvara and Peredonov are having a vicious argument but both remain calm throughout; they cannot even relate to each other in anger. Nor do Sologub's characters show any ability to exercise free will and develop. Except for Sasha, who has learned how to lust and lie, and for Peredonov who has lost his mind, all the characters are the same at the end of the novel as they were at the beginning.

Actually, such undynamic characters do have a place in realistic novels, but usually they play a very small role as foils for the principals. For example, there is the murdered pawnbroker who acts as Raskol'nikov's foil in *Crime and Punishment* or Evdoskaia Kukshina, the parodied feminist who prepares us for Odintsova in *Fathers and Sons*. Foster calls such characters "flat" and distinguishes them by the fact that they have no real existence outside the novel, according to him, whereas "round" characters, such as Moll Flanders, can be imagined living in the world.[2] The term "flat" can be usefully applied to all the characters in *The Petty Demon*, with the exception of Peredonov who will be considered separately. We cannot imagine any of them existing outside the novel because, lacking any feelings or ideals, they appear not to be genuine individuals but merely outcroppings of their world, and therefore dependent on each other and their environment for their very identities. Vershina, Peredonov's witchlike neighbor, would be unrecognizable without her fence, cigarettes, magic garden or her ward Marta whom she browbeats. For Marta to maintain her identity as a victim, she needs Perdonov and Vershina to abuse her. Varvara could not hatch her schemes without her friend Grushina to help her; similarly, Liudmila needs the bourgeoisie of the town to shock. Foster's term "flat" underlines the two-dimensional quality of Sologub's characters and helps account for the irritating effect they have on us. In creating a world entirely populated by flat characters, Sologub is suggesting that these are normal people and therefore that we, like them, are uninterested in ideals, feelings, or other people, and incapable of growth.

Sologub uses several devices to flatten his characters. First, he defines each character in the novel with one word or activity, to suggest that they are severely limited in their possibilities and incapable of any depth or development. Peredonov is usually gloomy (*ugriumyi*); Varvara often smirks (*ukhmyliaetsia*); Volodin, Peredonov's closest friend, is always described in terms of a sheep; Vershina stands by her gate and smokes, and so on.   Several characters are frankly described as machines:

> Peredonov and Ershova embraced and started to dance in the grass around the pear tree.   Peredonov's face, as before, remained dull and expressed nothing. His gold eyeglasses on his nose, and the short hair on his head, bounced mechanically as on an inanimate object. (69)

> This is the way Tishkov always talked [i.e., in rhymed couplets] if the conversation was not about him personally.   He would have bored everyone to death but they were used to him and no longer noticed his glibly delivered patter . . . .   But it was all the same to Tishkov whether people listened to him or not; he couldn't stop seizing others' words for rhyme and acted with the steadfastness of an intricately devised annoyance machine. (140)

> It was as if someone had extracted his [Kirillov's] living soul and put it in a long box and in its place inserted an inanimate but nimble fidgeting. (159)

If the characters always acted purely mechanically we would not consider them human at all and we would lose interest in them.   Very occasionally, however, Sologub has them show a small but disconcerting element of human feeling which draws attention to their flatness by showing the vast areas of their lives that they have renounced.   For example, Avinovitskii, the terrifying D.A., appears genuinely to love his son although he cannot show his feelings directly:

> Avinovitskii . . . looking at his son with a tenderness not at all in keeping with his thickly-bearded and angry face, said, "You, my boy, go tell her [the servant] to get us something to drink and eat."

> The boy unhurriedly left the sitting room.   His father looked at him with a proud and joyful smile. But when the boy was at the door Avinovitskii suddenly frowned and screamed in a voice so frightening that Peredonov started, "Quickly!"

> The *gimnaziia* student ran off . . . .   His   father

listened, smiled with his thick red lips and then spoke
again in an angry voice. "My heir. Nice — eh? How
will he turn out — eh? What do you think? He may
be a fool, but he'll never be a scoundrel, a coward or a
milksop." (144-45)

Although Varvara, too, usually acts like an automaton, one
description of her opinion about Peredonov makes her seem almost
pathetic. "She sincerely thought that he was good-looking and a
fine fellow. His stupidest actions seemed proper to her. To her he
was neither ridiculous nor repugnant" (71). These and other brief
moments of feeling make us look at the characters with a mixture
of horror and compassion that adds to the novel's repulsive but
compelling atmosphere.

A second device Sologub uses to flatten the characters is to
make them not only insensitive but impervious to each other. If,
as one critic said, the presentation of personal relationships is the
central interest of novels, then *The Petty Demon* is an anomaly in
this respect as well.[3]   There is never any meaningful exchange of
feelings nor do the characters even have much effect on each other
(with the exception of the children, who are still somewhat
vulnerable to cruelty). Instead, each character merely incorporates
others into his or her endlessly repeated activity — like gears in a
machine that mesh without ever interacting. What tension there is
in the novel arises from the unexpected resistance characters
encounter when the action they wish to perform involves other
people. Volodin is astounded when Nadezhda Adamenko does not
accept his proposal; Varvara is resolved to marry Peredonov by fair
means or foul and Peredonov only exists for her as an obstacle to
her desire; Peredonov is so out of touch with the people around
him that he imagines that he can attain the glory he craves by
proving that Sasha is a girl disguised as a boy. In treating others
as objects, the characters themselves become less than human.

Third, Sologub does not provide these characters with a
temporal dimension; they have no past, are unaffected by
experience, and have no future. In that they seem to exist outside
of time; change or growth is impossible for them. They cannot
think in the hypothetical mode; they never wonder about the
purpose of their lives, nor do they think of breaking out of their
society by leaving town or of changing their life in town in any
way. Their inability to change or even dream of change is one of
their least human aspects.

Only the children react spontaneously and creatively to situations, but it is clear that they will soon learn the deadened ways of adults. In one description of the town we are told, "There were people on the street and they walked slowly as if nothing motivated them to do anything, as if they could scarcely overcome their quiet drowsiness. Only the chldren, the eternal and unwearying vessels of God's joy on earth, were lively and ran and played. But already sluggishness lay its pall even on them and some faceless and invisible monster nestled behind their shoulders and peeped out from time to time through eyes full of menace at their suddenly dulled faces" (140-41).

Of course, realistic characters are not the only kind possible. Critics have gained considerable perspective on realism since the last century and now discuss it as a literary device, like any other, which an effective author uses for a definite purpose and not just for its own sake.[4] Sologub's characters, however, resemble neither the realistic norm nor the more isolated and cerebral but still sympathetic types of characters who succeeded them. Instead, in *The Petty Demon* the characters are just human enough to make reading the novel bearable. If we look at them functionally, however, they do serve several purposes: they keep us at a distance, prevent us from escaping into the novel through identification with them, and force us to look for meaning elsewhere in the novel. In addition, their flatness itself has significance because it is an expression of how they have dehumanized themselves through their petty behavior. Sologub may be suggesting that without the third dimension of relatedness, without an interest in something larger than one's self, whether religion, kindness to children or nature, life becomes empty and people become flat. Peredonov epitomizes this dilemma.

Protagonists of nineteenth-century realistic novels are generally flawed but sympathetic characters (Natasha Rostov, Raskol'nikov, Rastignac, Mme Bovary) who, in the course of the novel, learn something about life. Although the care Sologub lavishes on Peredonov, the detail with which we see him break down confers on him an importance that sets him apart from the rest of the characters, Peredonov is not the typical realistic protagonist, since in the course of the novel he becomes more and more enmired in illusion rather than freeing himself from it.

Peredonov is also unusual in that he is neither a round nor a flat character.   Certainly he lacks the complexity, spontaneity, and growth of heroes in the realistic tradition.   He is no more introspective than any of the other characters in the novel, responds to everything that happens to him with gloom and gets pleasure only from tormenting others.   Yet Peredonov does possess an archetypal power and, as we have seen, an ability to inspire compassion that sets him apart both from the other characters in the novel and from characters in other novels.   Peredonov's unusual effect on the reader becomes more understandable in the light of Edwin Muir's substitution of the terms "pure" and "dramatic" for Foster's "round" and "flat."   Pure characters, Muir writes (for example, Dickens' Mrs. Macawber), are static.   They talk and act only out of habit, never spontaneously, and therefore often seem ludicrous.   A dramatic character, in contrast, "breaks habit, or has it broken for him; he discovers the truth about himself, or in other words develops."[5]

In these terms Peredonov is neither flat nor round but exists in a kind of bas relief, a round character manqué.   The narrator describes Peredonov's unsuccessful attempts to develop in the following way:

> And after all, even Peredonov strove for the truth, according to the general law of all conscious life, and this striving tormented him.   He himself wasn't conscious that he, also, like all people strove for the truth and therefore his anxiety was undefined.   He couldn't find the truth for himself and so he had become entangled and was perishing. (345-46)

Peredonov is incapable of developing but has habit broken for him by madness.   He tries to discover the truth about himself, "striving toward truth according to the general law of all conscious life," and fails to discover it, "becomes entangled and perishes."   In contrast to tragic heroes who are always round and at least understand what they are fighting against and why they fail, Peredonov is flat, and the novel concerns his unconscious and unsuccessful struggle to become round.   It is just this unsuccessful struggle that interests us and excites our compassion and makes it possible for him to be the protagonist, although an unusual one.   As early as Chapter 6 we are told of the hopelessness of Peredonov's position: "But after all,

the bog Peredonov had crept into was a mirey one and no magic
charms would manage to plop him over into another" (111).
Because Peredonov does not understand that his problem is within,
he is unable to fight it effectively, but in any case, he can only
choose among bogs.

Peredonov stands apart both from the other characters in this
novel and from conventional realistic protagonists of other novels
by virtually embodying his world. He represents his world and is
central to it, just as Satan is at the center and bottom of Dante's
Inferno. Sologub makes clear in the introduction to the second
edition of the novel that Peredonov is the petty demon of the title:
" . . . it is about you that I have written my novel about the
Petty Demon and his terrible *nedotykomka*" (32). Since the
nedotykomka (which I will discuss in Chapter 6) is Peredonov's
private horror which no one else can see, the term "petty demon"
must refer to him.

In Peredonov we see an exaggeration of the pettiness and
gratuitous cruelty to the weak that characterizes his world, as well
as the source of much of that cruelty. In this world parents
routinely beat their children, Vershina mistreats Marta, Varvara
mistreats her servant, and people see others purely as objects.
Peredonov not only mistreats his students, his cat, his servant, and
all the women who want to marry him, but he also encourages
cruelty in others: he tells Volodin to tar Marta's gate (which is
understood to mean that she is not a virgin), Vladia to set Marta's
dress on fire, and he makes visits to parents, advising them to beat
their children.

Peredonov's breakdown dramatizes the problems of a society
that is cruel to the weak: there is great pressure to appear strong
even if one is not. At the beginning of the novel Peredonov seems
to be at the top of his world in his attractiveness to women and
his future prospects. The Rutilov sisters, Varvara, Marta and
Prepolovenskaia's cousin are all interested in marrying him, and
Peredonov feels he has a good chance of becoming a school
inspector. But all this only makes Peredonov insecure, not happy,
and leads him to attribute to other people his own envious and
petty feelings. At one point he thinks: "It's terrible to live among
envious and hostile people. But what can you do? They can't all
be inspectors. It's the struggle for existence!" (110). Peredonov's
power to attract women and command the respect of men is only

apparent, and he knows it. As soon as he chooses to marry any one woman, the rest will lose interest in him, and the only way he can get the job of inspector is by marrying Varvara, who makes him feel comfortable, but whom no one respects.

Peredonov's insecurity is reflected in his contempt for and fear of Pavel Volodin, supposedly his best friend. Everyone in the town ridicules Volodin, who cannot get any woman to marry him and has a lowly job as a shop teacher with no desire or hope of advancement. Rutilov emphasizes the contrast in social position between Volodin and Peredonov when he reassures Peredonov that his sisters would never make fun of him: "After all, you're not some sort of Pavlushka [Volodin] so that they would laugh at you" (81). But although Volodin is far below Peredonov in social standing, Peredonov is haunted by the fantasy that Volodin will kill him and usurp his position, marry Varvara, and become a school inspector. Even stranger, Peredonov is afraid that if Volodin replaced him no one would know the difference. On his wedding day he paints "P" all over his body for identification so that Volodin cannot take his place at the last moment. (Ironically the "P" for Peredonov could equally well stand for "Pavel.") These fears suggest that Peredonov unconsciously feels he is very much like Volodin in some ways, so like him as to be indistinguishable.

Volodin's double role as Peredonov's best friend and archenemy suggests that he represents for Peredonov an alter ego or *Doppelgänger*, the "loser" in himself that keeps him from succeeding. The symbol of success for Peredonov is getting the inspector's job: his whole feeling of worth as a human being depends on it and at one point he even thinks to himself, "How can I live if they don't give me the [inspector's] position?" (346). For Peredonov the job is symbolic of some kind of salvation. Because Peredonov is afraid of being unsuccessful like Volodin and cannot accept the Volodin within himself — the weak, foolish loser — he feels threatened by Volodin in the flesh. He translates his fear of being overwhelmed by the Volodin within him (a fear so great that he cannot even acknowledge it) into the delusion that Volodin wants to kill him. Ironically, it is Peredonov's very fear of being like Volodin that destroys him. He allows Varvara to trick him into marriage with two forged letters promising him the inspector's job. When Volodin tells Peredonov that Varvara has made a fool of him — that the Volodin within Peredonov has triumphed — Peredonov kills the external Volodin in what could almost be seen as a suicide. At no time during his breakdown can Peredonov ask anyone for help. He knows better than anyone how cruelly any weakness is treated in this society.

Chapter 5
Plot

Plot, or the structure of events in a novel, operates on two levels. The first, which may be called the macro-level, determines how the major subplots or story lines relate to each other, while the second, or micro-level, concerns the way one event leads to another within a particular story line. From the point of view of the first level — the interrelationship of plot lines — *The Petty Demon* somewhat resembles a well-crafted nineteenth-century realistic novel. As in *Anna Karenina*, for example, where the tragic principal plot concerning the unhappy Karenin family is offset by Levin's happier relationship with Kitty, in *The Petty Demon* there is a tragic major plot — Peredonov's developing madness — and an idyllic subplot concerning the erotic relationship between Sasha, a student of Peredonov's, and Liudmila.

Despite this similarity, however, the relationship between the story lines in these two novels is quite different, and it is worth considering how these differences affect the reader. While in *Anna Karenina* the two story lines have approximately equal weight, in *The Petty Demon* only five out of thirty-two chapters concern the Sasha-Liudmila subplot, and this leads the reader to consider it principally in relationship to Peredonov's story. In *Anna Karenina* the two story lines are more independent of each other. While contact between characters in the two stories occurs from time to time (the Levins and the Karenins are in the same social set), these sporadic meetings serve principally to highlight the contrast between a happy and an unhappy family. In *The Petty Demon*, however, the gradual convergence of the two story lines — i.e., Sasha's induction into Peredonov's world — is central to the novel; Sologub facilitates this convergence structurally by alternating the novel's two plots at an increasingly rapid rate. Thus Chapters 1-13 introduce Peredonov and his acquaintances, including Liudmila and Sasha. Chapter 14 describes Sasha's meeting with Liudmila, while Chapter 15 returns to Peredonov. The next two chapters (16 and 17) then describe the deepening relationship between

Liudmila and Sasha; subsequently Chapters 18 through 25 return to Peredonov, while Chapter 26 picks up with Sasha and Liudmila. Finally Chapters 27 to 32 play out the conflict between Peredonov and Sasha, a conflict in which Peredonov finally goes beserk and Sasha emerges triumphant.

Because the two plots of *The Petty Demon* are less equal in weight than those of *Anna Karenina*, it follows that Sologub moves between subplots somewhat differently from Tolstoy. In *Anna Karenina* the shifts are made either through mutual friendships or by simple juxtaposition. The first method works very smoothly; although the protagonists of the two plots—Levin and Anna Karenina—meet only once, there are many opportunities for contact between their circles. For example, Levin is a friend of Stepan's, Anna's brother, and is in love with Kitty, Anna's sister-in-law. Kitty (at least at the beginning of the novel) wants to marry Vronsky, who becomes Anna's lover. Dolly is both Anna's sister-in-law and Kitty's sister. Typically, Tolstoy devotes several chapters to one story line until a crisis arises and then, through a visit from a character involved in the other story line, he describes a parallel or contrasting development in the other plot. For example, in Book Six Dolly, who has been staying with Levin and Kitty, visits Anna, thus introducing the subsequent chapters concerning Anna's life with Vronsky. Sometimes the juxtaposition between the two plots is so clear that no interconnection is necessary. In Book 5, for example, the chapters describing Anna and Vronsky's first three months together in Europe are followed by a description of Levin and Kitty's first three months of marriage. Tolstoy's device of following one story up to a crisis and then shifting to the other one (as for example, in Book 2 when, at the beginning of Anna's affair with Vronsky, the narration suddenly returns to Levin) leaves the reader in considerable suspense; but one quickly gets caught up in the second story until at the most interesting point Tolstoy shifts back to the first.

In *The Petty Demon* the movement between plots is quite different. Instead of parallels arising from the contrasting way families react to common stresses, in Sologub's novel an infectious principle seems to operate, the two plots influencing each other by a kind of two-way osmosis. Liudmila's first contact with Sasha in Chapter 14, for example, follows immediately after Peredonov begins visiting his students and urging their parents to whip them. It is as if Liudmila's interest in Sasha is an outgrowth of

Peredonov's sadism. The next chapter, which concerns Volodin's proposal to Adamenko, ends with a quasi-erotic scene in which Adamenko tickles and punishes her younger brother (who is approximately Sasha's age), and the two rough-house on the floor. This scene seems both to have been influenced by Liudmila's pursuit of Sasha in the previous chapter, and to influence the two quasi-erotic chapters devoted to Sasha and Liudmila that follow. At the end of this section Liudmila brings Sasha to her room; she threatens him, locks the door, and Sasha becomes aware that the smell of her room reminds him of snakes. In the next chapter Peredonov, too, seems to act out of a combination of violence and eroticism. He arranges with Iulia Gudaevskaia to beat her son in her husband's absence, and as is implied in the text, and even more strongly in a deleted variant, goes to bed with her afterwards.[1] These mutual interactions between the two subplots increase in intensity. Chapter 25, describing Peredonov's growing insanity in thought and action is followed by a chapter describing Sasha's increasingly dark feelings toward Liudmila and then by one describing Peredonov's equally dark feelings toward Sasha. Of course Sologub, like Tolstoy, uses the shifts between story lines to create suspense; and as Tolstoy lightens the tragedy of the Karenins with Levin's happier marriage, so Sologub uses the eroticism of the Sasha-Liudmila subplot as a means of lightening the heaviness of Peredonov's story. Sologub differs from Tolstoy in the way he shifts between subplots. He does not make smooth transitions through characters' visits or establish objective comparisons of how a similar event affects the two stories, but uses associative links between chapters, links that break down and fragment traditional realistic assumptions. There is no rational reason why Peredonov's actions and mood should influence Liudmila or vice versa, and these mutual influences, although perhaps only unconsciously noticed by the reader, produce an uncanny and frightening effect. Furthermore, because of the increasingly frequent alternation between plot and subplot discussed above, these uncanny links between the plots also increase in frequency as the novel progresses; this adds to the reader's confused feeling that something is wrong that he cannot define and that he is an unwilling participant in the crescendo of Peredonovism and of madness.

Another strange device in *The Petty Demon* which is related to the play of story lines is the break of extra space between certain paragraphs starting with Chapter 12: Peredonov's visit to Sasha and the beginning of the Sasha-Liudmila subplot. From this point to the end of the novel every chapter is divided into at least two parts, one into as many as eleven parts, as if the bifurcation of plot were reflected in the fragmenting of the narrative. The spaces often separate characters' actions from their thoughts about their actions or divide scenes involving different characters. There is a space for example between Iulia's promise to send for Peredonov after her husband has left and the description of the note which arrives later that evening and Varvara's reactions to it. There is another space as the scene shifts to Peredonov's thoughts as he walks to Iulia's house.[2]

These divisions within chapters serve several functions. Most basically they represent a graphic breathing space which enables Sologub to shift among the large number of characters in Peredonov's circle. They also, however, affect our perception of the structure of events (the plot) by making the narrative seem discontinuous and elliptical; they suggest that we do not know everything there is to know about events, that something has been left out. Chapter 26, for example, which is devoted solely to Sasha and Liudmila's amourous explorations, is divided into eleven sections. By suggesting a succession of isolated moments or perhaps high points, these subdivisions give the chapter a power it would not have were it written as a unit. In this sense the spaces correspond to the three dots favored by symbolist poets to intimate the ineffable. One might even find an analogy with the mist in Gogol's short story "The Nose" which moves in to envelop everything at various points of the story, and thus forces the narrator to change the subject.

The meaning of the Sasha-Liudmila subplot, as suggested above, has been a matter of controversy. I do not agree with Blok that it represents a healthy pagan contrast with Peredonovism, nor with the reviewer who believed that in this subplot Sologub was trying to describe something pure and innocent but, because of his own debauched character, only succeeded in creating scenes of perversion.[3] Rather, I believe that the function of this subplot is to unmask another variety of Peredonovism: Sasha in his pivotal role in the two plots as both Peredonov's student, and also as the object of Liudmila's seductions, highlights similarities between Liudmila and Peredonov that otherwise would not be evident. These parallels are important because they suggest that no one, not even Liudmila—who considers herself a pagan and a lover of beauty and the human body—has escaped the pettiness and cruelty that taints everyone in the town.

Liudmila seems the very antithesis of Peredonov—charming, attractive and hedonistic instead of crude and dour; yet she and Peredonov victimize Sasha in similar ways. If Peredonov's sadistic behavior toward Sasha has erotic overtones, Liudmila's erotic behavior toward him is clearly characterized by sadistic elements. Liudmila has erotic dreams about Sasha in which he is whipped, and she teases him with puns which have violent innuendoes. She asks him if he wants her to *dushit'* (to scent or to smother) him, and if he likes *rozochki* (little roses or whipping rods). She demands complete obedience from him, undresses him against his will, and slaps him when she is displeased with him. Similarly, Peredonov tries to convince Sasha's landlady to beat him; he also has an erotic dream about the boy (Chapter 18).

Sologub underlines the similarities between Peredonov and Liudmila in the many parallels between the first visit each makes to Sasha (in Chapters 12 and 14). Both Peredonov and Liudmila go because they have heard the rumor that Sasha is a girl disguised as a boy; both find the thought intriguing and titillating and want to see if it is true. Both express immediate if indirect sexual interest in Sasha. Peredonov impatiently waits for Sasha's landlady to leave and then puts his arm around Sasha and tells him to confess that he is a girl. Liudmila, who is a little more circumspect, asks Sasha's landlady to find her a husband who looks like Sasha. Although Sasha reacts to Peredonov's visit with disgust and to Liudmila's with delight, in both cases he feels embarrassed. Another parallel between Peredonov and Liudmila is the way they grant favors. The scene in Chapter 17, in which Liudmila makes Sasha kiss her hand for every date she gives him, bears a striking resemblence to one in which Peredonov forces Varvara to kiss the hand that is making a "fig" at the top of his walking stick before he will give her money for the wedding (Chapter 23).

The juxtaposition of the two plots also establishes parallels between Peredonov and Sasha. The fact that each is the hero of a separate subplot, coupled with Peredonov's obsessive interest in Sasha, suggest that the latter is a Peredonov in the making—and that Liudmila, in awakening Sasha's sexuality, has taken him out of the pure world of children into the corrupt world of Peredonovian adults.

If *The Petty Demon* is somewhat unusual in the way the
subplots relate to each other, in respect to the second level of plot
I mentioned—the way one event leads to another within the
principal story line—the novel is decidely unique. Plots of realistic
novels, like those of plays, usually are based on conflicts between
characters or forces, and are structured according to Aristotelian
categories of dramatic development.   But, as I have already
indicated, characters in *The Petty Demon* do not struggle among
each other for conflicting goals because they have no goals, only
repeated actions.   Nor do Aristotelian categories apply. Instead we
have a bewildering series of events that fall into no apparent order
and are generated by no clear principle.   How, then, are events in
the novel structured?

   We can gain some insight into this problem by turning once
again to E. M. Forster's deceptively simple observations on the
novel.   Forster writes: "There are in novels two forces, human
beings and a bundle of various things not human beings, and . . .
it is the novelist's business to adjust these two forces and conciliate
their claims."   Forster also notes that "nearly all novels are feeble
in the end.   This is because the plot requires to be wound up."[4]
In order to do this, the writer must force his characters—who tend
to have a life of their own—to marry, die or reform.   What is
significant about these generalizations is that none of them applies
at all to the plot and characters of *The Petty Demon*.   First, the
characters in this novel are not fully human; and second, rather
than becoming feeble and less exciting at the end, *The Petty
Demon* gathers momentum throughout and culminates brilliantly in
a masquerade ball, a riot, a chase scene, a fire and a murder.

   Forster sheds some light on the peculiarity of *The Petty
Demon* when later in his book he describes the exception to his
rule: a small and unusual category which he calls "patterned
novels."   These are novels in which the plot can be summed up in
a pictorial or geometrical image, and in which character
development is secondary to such an externally imposed pattern.
As an example of this kind of novel Forster mentions *Roman
Pictures* by Percy Lubbock, which according to him has a "grand
chain" pattern; he also analyzes James's *The Ambassadors* as a
novel with an "hour glass" pattern.   Forster feels that the effect of
a rigid pattern on James's characters is to reduce them to
"maimed specialized creatures" and his final verdict on such novels

is that they are "beautifully done, but not worth doing."[5]

While I do not agree with Forster's view of *The Ambassadors* or believe that *The Petty Demon* could be usefully classified with both this novel and *Roman Pictures* as members of one subgenre, I do find Forster's term, "patterned novel," very illuminating when applied to *The Petty Demon*. Certainly the inhabitants of Peredonov's world could be described as "maimed, specialized creatures": Vershina does nothing but smoke and lure passersby into her garden, Tishkov speaks only in rhyme, and Peredonov, being defective in a defective world, is doubly maimed. Furthermore, Forster's term explains the accelerating tempo of events in the novel, as well as the principle by which these otherwise chaotic events may be linked; they are part of a pattern, a "crescendo" or theme and variation pattern that corresponds to Peredonov's growing insanity. To use another image, events in the novel can be seen as expanding ripples that emanate from a few stones cast by Sologub at various points in the novel.

Ideas, incidents, characters and even objects that Sologub introduces early in the novel recur again and again, transformed into larger, more ornate and more frightening forms as Peredonov goes mad. Fire, which appears in the epigraph of the novel ("I wished to burn her, the wicked witch") is only one example of this elaboration. In Chapter 5 Peredonov burns some books he considers subversive; he speculates in Chapter 12 that when people die their houses should be burned. In Chapter 22 he recounts that he has advised Marta's brother to set fire to her dress and when he burns a deck of cards in Chapter 25 he sees the princess emerge from it. In the apocalyptic ending of the novel Peredonov loses all hold on reality and burns down the community hall in which the masquerade ball has taken place. The princess, who is introduced at the beginning of the novel as Varvara's benefactor appears to Peredonov in ever more frightening forms. She is transmogrified in Peredonov's mind in the course of the novel into Peredonov's savior, Pushkin's Queen of Spades, a vile old woman who demands Peredonov denounce all his friends and become her lover, a spy, and finally a personification of death "cold and distant." Peredonov's cat undergoes a similarly terrifying metamorphosis in Peredonov's mind. It starts to hiss and scratch at Peredonov, then mysteriously runs away for a few days and returns. Perhaps this is an allusion to Gogol's "Starosvetskie pomeshchiki" ("Old-Fashioned Landowners") in which a cat runs away and returns as a harbinger of death. Later Peredonov's cat looks at him evilly when Peredonov falsely accuses his maid of stealing some raisins and Peredonov thinks the cat is like a werewolf. At Peredonov's wedding the cat appears to Peredonov to have been transformed into a man with a red mustache, and afterwards Peredonov takes it to the barber to be shaved. On several occasions Peredonov connects the malevolence of the cat with the appearance of the *nedotykomka*, his private horror. Perhaps Peredonov connects the cat with the *nedotykomka* because both act independently of him and yet belong to him. The *nedotykomka* is like a ghastly pet that torments him and that he cannot get rid of.

Many other events are organized by this crescendo or theme-and-variation pattern. At the beginning of the novel Peredonov besmirches a wall and at the end he believes it hides an enemy. Knives become more and more frightening to Peredonov. He screams at Varvara to put one down in Chapter 5, eventually refuses to use them at all, and has Varvara cook soft foods that do not have to be cut. In the end, of course, Peredonov uses a knife to kill Volodin. Some of the themes and variations are humorous. In Chapter 19, for example, Volodin tells Peredonov to watch out that his glasses do not burst and the next night Gudaevskii, angry that his son has been beaten, punches Peredonov and breaks his glasses.

The effect of this crescendo pattern on the reader is most disorienting. As the same objects keep reappearing in increasingly frightening forms one begins to experience a sense of déjà vu, inevitability and even inexorable doom that is qualitatively similar to Peredonov's feelings. This is because while Peredonov is trying to make sense of these events physically, we are trying to make sense of them aesthetically by fitting them into some conventional novelistic structure. The events, however, simply do not make sense in a realistic context and so we, like Peredonov, continue to struggle with them; we continue only because the half-perceived pattern convinces us that the events are not random, that there is some organizing principle at work which we simply have not grasped. This tantalizing struggle to make sense out of a subtly organized chaos is what, in large part, I believe, keeps us reading the novel. We consequently read *The Petty Demon* far more actively than we would a realistic novel, looking for the key to events.

These patterns, however, and the principle that generates them, cannot be thoroughly understood in isolation. In *The Petty Demon*, which concerns a man going mad, plot—the structure of events—merges with character. That is, Peredonov creates his own reality out of his mad perception of the world and thus generates the novel's pattern. Although he does not realize it, Peredonov is the direct or indirect cause of his own and other's suffering. To understand the meaning of this pattern of events, then, it is necessary to get a better understanding of Peredonov and the vicious circles of thought and being in which he is trapped. The implications of Peredonov's problems extend beyond both his character and the events he instigates. For Peredonov is representative of both the novelistic world he inhabits and of what Sologub feels is wrong with our world. A consideration of the ways in which Peredonov generates the pattern of events in the novel, therefore, will lead us to an understanding of the self-destructive qualities of Peredonovism in general.

Chapter 6
The Pattern of Peredonovism

I have said the events in *The Petty Demon* are organized by a pattern of escalating intensity rather than by an Aristotelian plot. In reading the novel our subliminal awareness of this peculiarity inspires strong and contradictory feelings; irritation mixes with satisfaction, depression with delight. We are simultaneously annoyed because Sologub frustrates our expectation of a conventional plot, yet appeased because he provides us—through the pattern itself—with a strong sense of inevitability and resolution when the novel ends.

The entire crescendo pattern is the result of the operation within the novel of a single diabolical principle: the creation of misery for oneself through cruelty to others. This force generates, moves, and connects all the events within the world of the novel as invisibly and as powerfully as the law of gravity controls objects. I have referred to this force as Peredonovism, because it is in Peredonov, the petty demon himself, that we see both its most extreme form and its logical culmination in madness. It is my contention, then, that unknowingly, Peredonov himself generates the novel's crescendo pattern, that he is directly or indirectly responsible for most of the increasingly unpleasant events that happen to him. Peredonovism, however, is a very complex phenomenon; in order to understand its operation in the novel, we must consider its various levels.

On the most obvious level, Peredonov creates misery for himself and others through the operation of the law of cause and effect. That is, much of the hostility directed against Peredonov, which he thinks is gratuitous, represents the anger or retaliation of those he has previously mistreated. As in the Hindu law of negative karma, Peredonov's petty actions come back to haunt him as his "fate." Peredonov's cat hisses at him and behaves peculiarly because Peredonov often rubs it with thistles, blows in its ears, and rubs its fur the wrong way for amusement. Varvara tricks Peredonov into marrying her, and later, when he wants sympathy, teases him and uses his fears against him in order to pay him back for his cruel treatment of her before their marriage when he beat her, spat on her, stayed away nights, and threatened to throw her out by marrying Marta. The sudden delivery just before a housewarming party of Peredonov's old hat—an event which frightens him considerably—represents the revenge of his former landlady; after Peredonov had messed up the apartment and left without giving the landlady any notice, she had the hat he left behind cursed by a gypsy and returned to him. It is not surprising either that Gudaevskii punches Peredonov and breaks his glasses after Peredonov, with the help of Gudaevskii's wife, secretly beats their son. Similarly, Kramarenko follows Peredonov after school and calls him names after Peredonov has him beaten by his parents for no reason at all. Peredonov does not seem to realize that there is a connection between the way he behaves toward others and their reactions toward him.

Several factors cause these acts of retaliation to increase as the novel progresses: Peredonov becomes more sadistic as he breaks down and thus evokes fiercer reactions from the people he hurts; after he marries Varvara (in Chapter 23) he loses his exalted status as an eligible bachelor and becomes inconsequential in the eyes of women who wanted to marry him and they, no longer having anything to lose, vent their wounded vanity on him. Prepolovenskaia, who wanted her niece to marry Peredonov, sends him anonymous and threatening letters; Vershina, who wanted him to marry Marta, frightens him with dark hints; and the Rutilov sisters, all of whom he rejected, mock him. Finally, as Varvara's forged letter and Peredonov's growing madness become known in the town, people turn on him and attack him simply because he is vulnerable. "Already even acquaintances were starting to tease Peredonov about being fooled [by Varvara]. With the insensitivity toward the weak usual in our town they spoke about the deception right in front of him" (346).

Even this cruelty to Peredonov represents the working of cause and effect. Before marrying Varvara, Peredonov played all the women who wanted to marry him against each other, and throughout the novel he consistently mistreats vulnerable characters such as Marta and her brother Vladia.

On a deeper, epistomological level, Peredonov causes increasingly unpleasant events to happen to him through his inability to distinguish among thoughts, words, and the things they symbolize. This confusion causes Peredonov to project the growing chaos in his mind out onto his world and he begins to mistake his own thoughts for objective truth. At the beginning of the novel, for example, when Rutilov, an acquaintance, first suggests that Peredonov marry one of his sisters, Peredonov tells him he is afraid Varvara will poison him if he does not marry her. This fear has no basis in fact, given Varvara's bovine character. When he goes home, however, Peredonov takes his own paranoid thoughts for reality and accuses Varvara of poisoning his tea. Similarly, when Volodin tells Peredonov about a new dish he would like to make for him, Peredonov credits Volodin with the envy he would feel if their positions were reversed, and becomes convinced that Volodin, too, wants to poison him so he can marry Varvara. Peredonov's belief that Volodin and Varvara want to poison him grows in force throughout the novel and becomes the underlying theme of his madness.

Peredonov also does not distinguish between words and objective truth, and so he assumes that anything people say is true, no matter how silly. When Varvara tells him Grushina's ridiculous idea that Sasha is really a girl in disguise, Peredonov believes her and even a visit to Sasha cannot shake this belief. Peredonov's refusal to understand that Sasha is a boy even when this has been proven, makes him a laughing stock in the town. But he persists, believing that he will not only be promoted but decorated for informing the authorities of this supposed scandal.

There are other instances of Peredonov's automatic and misguided acceptance of words. When Rutilov and Grushina, for their own petty reasons, tell Peredonov that the *gimnaziia* students misbehave at home, Peredonov believes them and later decides to gain even more recognition from the authorities by visiting students at home to discover their wrongdoings. When he fails to discover any he nonetheless tells the parents that their children have been misbehaving and advises that they be beaten. What he had done, in effect, was to confuse Grushina's and Rutilov's allegations with his own fantasies of being decorated by the government, and his sadistic enjoyment in tormenting children. Complaints about Peredonov's behavior eventually reach the headmaster and contribute to the latter's decision to suspend Peredonov.

In general, Peredonov, who is often described as *tupoi*, or dull, lacks the intelligence, humor, and aesthetic sense to distinguish between figurative and literal levels of language.   For example, when the narrator describes Volodin as being like a lamb he is using a humorous figure of speech and the reader can enjoy the simile:

> In the hall a bleating like a sheep's voice was heard
> . . . With a joyful, loud laugh Pavel Vasil'evich Volodin
> entered, a young man whose face and manner bore an
> amazing resemblance to a lamb: his hair was curly like
> a lamb's, his eyes were bulging and vacant.   In
> everything he was like a cheerful lamb—a stupid young
> man. (55)

Peredonov, however, is convinced that Volodin actually is a lamb, and one that is both predatory and dangerous.   He eventually acts on his fear, and realizes the simile by slitting Volodin's throat in a murder that is reminiscent of an animal sacrifice.   Peredonov's confusion of thoughts, words, and facts makes it impossible for him to distinguish between the nightmare inside his head and the petty but somewhat less terrifying reality around him.

The third and deepest level of Peredonovism is also the source of the other two: Peredonov rejects his true nature.   He is terrified of the very things that would free him from his defensive, gloomy, non-responsiveness to life, and from the deadness and insensitivity with which he isolates himself from others.   Sologub says about Peredonov: "For him, being happy meant doing nothing and, isolated from the world, gratifying his belly" (141).   That is, Peredonov wants a life with no risks, no giving, no pain and total security—a life that is impossible outside the womb.   Inevitably people often confront Peredonov with requests that he give of himself to others and risk pain and insecurity.   Peredonov refuses because he is afraid to become vulnerable to pain, afraid to admit that he has weaknesses.   That would mean being like the others, like Volodin, for example.   Peredonov thus reacts to any kind of demand with fright and feelings of persecution; he even fears those people and things that would bring him out of himself.

To isolate himself from others' demands, Peredonov blankets himself in gloom, moroseness, and insensitivity and suppresses his potential responsiveness, gaiety, spontaneity and affection.   But once "safe" from others, Peredonov feels isolated and lonely:

> On the way he sadly thought that everywhere, always,

people did nothing but laugh at him.   No one wanted
to help him.   Anguish oppressed his heart.   (324)

If   only   someone   would   deliver   him   [from   the
nedotykomka]   with some word or with a backhand blow.
But he had no friends here, no one would come to save
him.   He had to figure out his own way before the
venomous thing destroyed him.   (341-42)

Peredonov's self-protective withdrawal from others, his offensive
defense, leads to total isolation and constricts his life to the point
of madness.   For without people and things to relate to, without
an external reality to check his ideas against, he is at the mercy of
his fantasies and no longer knows what is real.   Peredonov has
won a Pyrrhic victory.   In order to protect himself so that he can
live, he has sacrificed almost everything that makes life meaningful.
His situation is what R. D. Laing calls a "double bind."[1]   He
cannot stand either to relate to people or not to relate to them.
In existential terms Peredonov is afraid to make contact with "the
other" in any form (i.e., anything not under his control).   Not
being able to admit he is afraid of "the other," Peredonov becomes
hostile and tries to destroy it.   But because a part of him wants
and needs relationships, it perpetually haunts him.

Peredonov could break out of his isolation and make contact
with others in many ways—through nature, religion, children,
women or art.   But he rejects them all repeatedly and as he
retreats further into his delusions, they become increasingly
threatening to him; he, in turn, becomes even more frightened and
withdrawn, establishing a vicious circle.   This vicious circle ends in
madness and is at the basis of the novel's crescendo-like pattern.
Peredonov's struggle with these manifestations of "the other" also
determines much of the content of his delusions.

Nature

Instead of giving himself up to an appreciation of nature as
something greater than himself, throughout the novel Peredonov
attributes to it his own hostility and petty feelings.   Thus, instead
of renewal and regeneration, he experiences only gloom.   As
Sologub writes, "Peredonov felt in nature the reflections of his own
anguish, of his own fears in the form of its hostility toward him.
That   inner   life   in   all   nature—inaccessible   to   objective

definition—that life which alone creates true, deep, and indubitable relations between man and nature—that life he didn't feel. For this reason all of nature seemed to him imbued with petty human feelings" (310-11).

As Peredonov deteriorates, he perceives the weather and other aspects of nature in increasingly menacing terms. As he drives to his wedding he feels that the trees refuse to give shade, and that the sun is spying on him from behind a cloud. This may be an indirect expression of his doubts about his marriage. After his wedding he begins to see nature as even more actively hostile and sinister:

> A little cloud wandered around the sky, roamed, sneaked about (clouds wear soft shoes) and spied on him. On its dark edges a dark gleam smiled mysteriously. Above the river, which flowed between the park and the town, the shadows of houses and bushes wavered and whispered, looking for somebody. (326)

In the final stage of his madness, Peredonov projects on nature the enemy within—his own Volodin-like characteristics which he despises and denies—and sees Volodin in a lamb-shaped cloud that he thinks is following him.

Peredonov extends his hostility toward nature to the animal kingdom and torments his cat. He is not even capable of giving this independent creature the small amount of affection it needs. Then, perhaps in anger at what he feels are the cat's unreasonable demands, or perhaps out of a feeling of guilt for his mistreatment of the animal, he comes to see it as an enemy.

Peredonov not only personifies nature as hostile, but blurs the boundaries between humans and animals. He sees both men and animals as enemies: "Everything was blended into a general hostility toward Peredonov. Dogs laughed at him, people barked at him" (326). His cat is transformed into a man and his closest friend Volodin into a sheep; both, he feels, are deadly enemies. Peredonov sees everything outside himself as hostile, spying, seeking to destroy him. Ironically, in his rejection of any relationship with nature, Peredonov returns to primitive, animistic thinking, which attributes a soul to everything in nature, an affirmation of nature's power.

CHAPTER 6

Religion

Religion might also release Peredonov from his isolation, but he reacts to it as he does to nature; he refuses to open himself and consequently finds religion threatening. The narrator tells us:

> The Church service, so close to such a multitude of people, not in its words and rites, but in its innermost movement, was incomprehensible to Peredonov and therefore frightening to him. The swinging of the censors terrified him as though it were mysterious sorcery . . . . The secret of eternal transubstantiation of impotent matter into a force that dissolves the bonds of death was forever hidden from him. (299–300)

Peredonov is frightened by the service because he does not understand it and because he is afraid of feelings of religious communion which make him feel vulnerable and threaten his isolation. If Peredonov were truly unreligious he would be indifferent to, rather than afraid of, the service. This contention is borne out by the connection between religion and the *nedotykomka*.

The latter, Peredonov's private horror, first appears to him during the blessing of his new apartment (Chapter 12) at a moment when, the narrator tells us, Peredonov is feeling as if he were a believer. It later torments him in church and during his wedding ceremony. The *nedotykomka*, which Peredonov alone can see, symbolizes his withdrawal from God's world into a hell of his own making. In keeping others away, Peredonov has imprisoned himself and created his own torturer. The presence of the *nedotykomka*, especially in church where one of the most basic forms of communion with "the other" takes place, is a painful reminder to Peredonov of what he has given up. Peredonov, one feels, is potentially a religious person, but fear cuts him off from this source of consolation.

For religion, in which one surrenders the will to something greater than oneself, Peredonov substitutes magic, the manipulation of language and objects for one's own ends. Peredonov avoids contact with others by drawing magic circles around himself and reciting magic spells so that he will not be bewitched (i.e., influenced by others). The *nedotykomka*, described as gray and spherical, represents a three-dimensional magic circle. *Tykat'* means both "to poke or jab" and "to address on an intimate basis." The *nedotykomka* (which might be roughly translated as the creature which does not allow itself to be touched or penetrated beyond a certain point) is the objectification of Peredonov's inability to drop his defenses and enjoy any form of intimacy.

Peredonov actually attends church more often as he becomes more isolated because he is afraid of authority and wants to placate both the heavenly powers and those that determine social opinion in the town. In a childish way he believes that if he is "good" (i.e., behaves himself) he will be given the inspector's job and going to church is one very conspicuous way of being good. Peredonov tries to appear good because he doubts that he is good by nature; he unconsciously expresses his conviction that he is evil by his fear that he will be denounced (which prompts him to denounce others first), and by abasing himself before figures of authority. Self-abasement and denunciations of others, he thinks, are what the authorities require of him for the inspector's job.

In church Peredonov principally responds to other people's outward behavior. He becomes extremely sensitive to anything less than perfect decorum among the students and reports what he considers inappropriate dress for his fellow teachers to Bogdanov, the school inspector (Chapters 7 and 22). This is another way for him to curry favor with the authorities. Later, for similar reasons, Peredonov will write denunciations of everyone he knows to placate the Princess. The people whom Peredonov considers authorities—policemen, the prosecutor, the mayor, the school inspector, etc.—have no idea why Peredonov acts the way he does and are merely confused by his behavior. In Chapter 21, for example, he bewilders a policeman by asking permission to smoke. On being told that there is no law against smoking he throws away his cigarette anyway because there is no law specifically allowing it.

Children

The children Peredonov teaches could offer him still another source of communion. Childhood had a special meaning for Sologub, who believed that sexual awareness did not begin until puberty, and who called pre-pubescent children "the eternal unwearying vessels of God's joy on earth." Like nature, then, young children in this novel are qualitatively different and essentially purer than adults. Peredonov in his classes, however, prefers the slovenly students and picks on the "clean" ones (141). He treats as equals "only those students who shaved and in whom an attraction to women was awakening" (178). This suggests that slovenliness in this novel is linked with puberty while cleanliness and purity are associated with young children.

Peredonov is afraid of the young boys he rejects, either because he secretly feels attracted to their innocence (but is afraid to care about them), or because he feels guilty about how he has mistreated them. He is afraid that both Misha (Chapter 15) and Kramarenko (Chapter 19) will bite him, possibly an inversion of his own oral violence (verbal abuse) toward them. At the end of the novel the eights in Peredonov's deck of cards are transformed in his mind into little boys with hooved legs and whipping rods for tails. Again, Peredonov, who does the whipping, has attributed his violence to his victims.

Sasha, who moves from innocence to sexual awareness in the course of the novel, is the child toward whom Peredonov feels the greatest ambivalence. Peredonov first notices Sasha when Varvara claims the latter is a girl in disguise. This rumor establishes Sasha in Peredonov's mind as a sexual being and thus piques Peredonov's interest. When Peredonov sees Sasha pray in church, Sasha's innocence and genuine religious feelings arouse only sexual and sadistic feelings in Peredonov:

> Peredonov observed him and felt it was particularly pleasant when Sasha knelt like someone being punished and looked ahead to the shining altar doors with an anxious and pleading expression on his face. There was supplication and sadness in his black eyes which were overshadowed by long, blue-black lashes. He was dark, well-proportioned (this was especially noticeable when he knelt peacefully and erectly as if under someone's stern, observing gaze) with a high and broad chest. He seemed to Peredonov just like a girl. (178)

Both Peredonov's pleasure at the thought of Sasha's being punished, and his enjoyment in tormenting his students suggest that he is sexually attracted to them but cannot admit it to himself. He uses sadism as both a substitute for sex and a screen, a way of hiding from himself his sexual feeling for boys. His rationale is that if he is cruel to boys he cannot be attracted to them.   The rumor that Sasha is a girl allows Peredonov for the first time to experience his sexual feelings for a boy under the pretense of heterosexuality.   Peredonov's attraction to Sasha can be seen in the way he admires the boy's appearance in church, visits him, puts him arm around him and dreams about him. Peredonov's inability to accept the fact that Sasha is a boy may stem from his need to justify his attraction to him in heterosexual terms.

But even in heterosexual terms Peredonov is not completely comfortable with his feelings toward Sasha.   He needs not only to believe that Sasha is a girl, but that he is an evil girl who plans to seduce all the *gimnaziia* students.   Peredonov does not want to accept responsibility for his own attraction to Sasha and it is more comfortable for him to blame everything on Sasha's evil plan. Thus, Peredonov dreams that Sasha is seducing him: "Peredonov had a nasty and terrible dream.   [Sasha] Pyl'nikov came, stood in the doorway, beckoned, and smiled.   It was as if someone was pulling Peredonov toward him and Pyl'nikov led him along dark, dirty streets, and the cat ran beside them, and its green pupils shone" (261).

Subsequently Peredonov falls back on theories of witchcraft, and rather than accept the fact that Sasha is a boy, prefers to believe that he is simultaneously a boy and a girl: "Sasha's face was tormenting and seductive to Peredonov.   The damned little boy was bewitching him with his insidious smile.   But was he in fact a little boy?   Or perhaps there were two of them: a brother and a sister.   And you couldn't sort out which one was where.   Or maybe it was even possible that he could switch from a boy to a girl.   It was not without reason that he was always so clean. When he switched he rinsed himself in various magic waters—otherwise, of course, he couldn't do it—he wouldn't change" (364).

Behind Peredonov's denial of his sexual feelings toward boys, however, there is still another level of denial.   Paradoxically, Peredonov's sexual feelings serve to distance him from his students. If he sees boys as sexual objects he can spend his energy denying his sexual feelings by being sadistic.   In this way he does not have to relate to the boys on their own terms, as non-sexual beings and as something different from himself.   By reducing boys to sexual objects Peredonov keeps his relationship with them under control.

Women

Outwardly, at least, Peredonov seems heterosexual, and the fourth possible way out of isolation that Peredonov rejects is through relationships with women. Peredonov mistrusts women in general and attributes great power and evil motives to them. He thinks Varvara wants to poison him and marry Volodin, and that she can bewitch him; he also thinks that Grushina wants to blackmail him, that the Rutilov sisters will laugh at him, that Marta wants to trap him into marrying her, and that the princess will either save or destroy him. The epigraph of the novel ("I wished to burn her, the wicked witch") seems to refer to the scene in Chapter 25 in which Peredonov throws a deck of cards into the fire and sees the princess emerge from the flames. Yet the epigraph describes Peredonov's attitude toward all women, for he sees them all as witches. In other words, he feels manipulated by women and believes they are stronger then he.

Peredonov does enjoy the prestige of having many women interested in him and the opportunities to satisfy his sexual desires. But perhaps because he senses that many of the women are only interested in him because of his good salary and expectations of becoming a school inspector, Peredonov often finds women's attraction to him a source of anxiety. Even more frightening to Peredonov, however, is that women may, like animals and children, demand respect and emotional commitment from him. He is afraid to marry any of the Rutilov sisters because none of them would have to take the initiative in a relationship with him. He is more comfortable with women who pursue him (such as Varvara and Iulia Gudaevskaia). With these women he can fulfill his sexual needs without having to express any positive feelings or make any emotional commitment.

There are two reasons why Peredonov fears and rejects women. His fear stems firstly from a denial of part of himself—the nurturing, sensitive, creative and powerful female principle which he has suppressed in order to deny his weaknesses. Thus, feeling alienated from the feminine side of his nature, Peredonov is threatened by women in general. Secondly his sexual attraction to women (Varvara, Marta, the Rutilov sisters) makes him feel vulnerable to them and thus gives them great power over him. If he approaches them, they may ridicule or reject him, something Peredonov's fragile self-esteem will not tolerate. He therefore treats them as objects, rejecting them before they can reject him. He turns down all three of the Rutilov sisters and treats both Varvara and Marta with contempt. However, he is really very insecure and vulnerable to rejection as can be seen both by his unrealistic fear that Varvara and Volodin want to kill him so they can marry, and his equally unreasonable jealousy of Murin, Marta's suitor (Chapter 19), particularly since by this time Peredonov has decided to marry Varvara.

Clearly Peredonov is the unconscious cause of his own unhappiness; it is he who prompts Varvara's betrayal of him, bringing about the very ridicule he fears. He puts so much pressure on Varvara (by threatening to marry someone else unless the princess helps him) that she forges a letter from the princess to keep him quiet. His pride will not allow him to see that both this letter and a subsequent one are fakes. And when, after he marries Varvara, the truth comes out, the entire town laughs at him.

Nevertheless, Peredonov is aware to some degree that Varvara is fooling him. The series of visits he makes to prominent people in the town to get protection from imaginary "enemies" are a reaction to his suppressed doubts about the authenticity of the first letter. As Sologub writes, "But Peredonov didn't know whether to believe [the letter] or not. In any case he decided to begin his self-vindicating visits to the important people in the town on Tuesday. He couldn't start on Monday—it was an unlucky day" (128).

Peredonov's visits are not only useless but damaging to his career. In trying to get protection from his enemies, he merely convinces the people he visits that everyone is gossiping about him; also he often betrays his most shameful secrets. For example, he tells the mayor

> "They talk all kinds rubbish. They claim that I tell the students dirty stories but that's garbage. Of course, sometimes you tell something funny in class in order to liven it up . . . . They say even worse things about me . . . that I live with Varvara. They say she isn't my cousin but my mistress. But, honest to God, she is my cousin, only very far removed, a third cousin, so we can marry. And we are getting married . . . ." (133–34)

These visits, though they damage Peredonov's career, serve several psychological functions: they are his way of placating what are to him frightening authority figures (the mayor, the chief of police, etc.); they are also disguised cries for help; they allow him to express his doubts about Varvara by projecting them onto his "enemies"; they give him a chance to boast about his career, making him feel more secure; and, most important, they give him something to do so that he does not have time to think.

His doubts about Varvara are also indicated by his speculation that she is carrying the *nedotykomka* in her pocket (Chapter 12), from which she took the first of the forged letters she gave him. As time goes on, he grows increasingly paranoid and is convinced that Varvara is a witch. Ultimately he believes she is capable of bewitching him both with or without the use of cards. Although he hints several times to her that he suspects that she has forged the letters, he never actually comes to grips with his doubts because he desperately wants to believe that the letters are genuine. The witchery with which Peredonov invests Varvara is a reflection of his own ability to fool himself.

Women for Peredonov, then, are objects of profound ambivalance; for him they are preservers as well as destroyers to whom he attributes great power. He sees the princess as his only chance for salvation and feels safe walking home after a party because Varvara is with him. On his wedding day he puts on rouge and wants to borrow Varvara's corset, trying, it would seem, symbolically to invoke her power to protect him. But women will not protect him because Peredonov is caught in another vicious circle. Being alienated from the female part of himself, he attributes great powers to women, is afraid of them, and mistreats them in order to hide his fear. But his behavior only makes the women retaliate and mistreat him in turn, thereby heightening his fear of them.

Art

Finally, Peredonov also rejects art as a way out of his self-imposed isolation. With the lovely piano music that momentarily soothes Peredonov while he waits in front of Rutilov's house (Chapter 4) Sologub suggests that art has healing power. But the music quickly ceases to have any effect because Peredonov grows irritated and stops listening to it. Although he teaches Russian literature in the *gimnaziia*, the idea that a work of art establishes communication between an artist and his audience is beyond Peredonov, who cannot communicate with anyone. In any case, his inability to distinguish between the literal and the figurative (which I discussed earlier) makes it impossible for him to enjoy literature on its own terms. Instead, he incorporates whatever he reads into his warped sense of reality. For example, when he and his class read a Krylov fable about a boasting traveler who is told about a bridge that throws liars into the water (Chapter 24), Peredonov does not think to abstract from the fable a generalized meaning. Instead, he believes the story literally and since he himself has been telling lies about the princess, he becomes afraid of the bridge in his town. Similarly, he imposes his own wish to dominate Varvara on a Pushkin poem about a wolf who, followed by his hungry mate, sets out at dawn. The meaning of this stanza, he tells his class, is that a woman must always follow and eat after her husband (Chapter 27). Peredonov is so self-absorbed and self-defensive that he is incapable of understanding any artistic reference; he simply takes everything literally and personally.

Indeed, in *The Petty Demon* Peredonov functions as a kind of anti-artist, creating ugliness, unhappiness and self-isolation instead of beauty, pleasure, and communion. In this sense, one could say that Peredonov expresses himself in many artistic media. He "paints" by besmirching his landlady's walls and when he dances (Chapters 3, 21, 25) the results are grotesque and zombielike. As for his literary efforts, they take the form of written denunciations of all his friends and acquaintances to the police.

Perhaps his greatest negative art work, however, is his madness, the apocalyptic nightmare he creates in his mind for himself and everyone around him. In fact, there are parallels between Peredonov's madness and art. Art can be a way of transcending everyday events in search of a higher and more general truth, and toward the end of the novel Peredonov becomes convinced that a higher truth exists, a truth which other people in town know nothing about:

"Who were you whispering to?" Peredonov asked mournfully.

Varvara smirked and answered. "But Ardal'on Borisych, it just seemed like that to you."

"Not everything just seems," Peredonov muttered sadly, "there is also truth on earth." (345)

"I spit on your truth," answered Peredonov [to
Vershina], "I spit on it thoroughly." (411)

The similarities between madness and art, however, exist only
on the surface.   While the horror and chaos of Peredonov's mad
world convince him that there must be a better one somewhere
else, his madness does not help him reach the truth.   Rather, it
isolates him and thus keeps him from the very communion with
others that would lead to the truth he seeks.   Art, unlike madness,
is a voluntary and conscious activity.   There has to be a difference
between the artist and his creation or in J. R.   Tolkien's terms,
between the primary world of reality and the secondary world of
art.[2]   Peredonov, completely at the mercy of his delusions, is
incapable of making such distinctions and so cannot be considered
an artist.

To a lesser degree than Peredonov, the others in the town
also devote themselves to the creation of ugliness and unhappiness.
In a passage cited below the narrator vividly describes how Dar'ia's
drunken caterwauling destroys the beautiful Russian song she is
singing.   Similarly, Varvara and Grushina, the narrator shows us,
destroy the beauty of their bodies:

> Although Varvara staggered with drunkenness and her
> face would have inspired revulsion in any pure person
> with its flabby and lascivious expression, her body was
> beautiful, like the body of a gentle nymph which had
> attached to it, by the force of some despicable spell, the
> head of a fading whore. (102)

> Everything that Grushina so boldly displayed in her
> skimpy costume was beautiful.   But what contradictions.
> She had fleabites on her skin, her manners were coarse,
> her words were unbearably banal.   Once again, profaned
> bodily beauty. (380-81)

Liudmila, with her love of brightly-colored clothing, exotic
perfumes, and her fascination with the human body, is the only
person in the town concerned with creating beauty.   Nonetheless
she is a *fleur du mal*.   Her perfumes remind Sasha of snakes,
bedbugs, and spiders; her dreams are of sultry and exotic settings
filled with whippings and cruelty; and her beautiful clothing
transforms Sasha for the night of the costume ball into a girl, a
realization of Grushina's most spiteful rumor.   Liudmila uses her
personal attractiveness to get power over and torment Sasha, and

to titillate herself.

The hostility of the people of the town to beauty, along with their greed, pettiness, and envy, is epitomized in the events that take place on the night of the ball. The local actors, the only artists in the town, decide to hold a masquerade and give prizes for the best costumes. The townspeople, however, are incapable of enjoying the ball for its own sake, but are only concerned with the prizes. When these turn out to be of no material value, they blame the actors but remain just as eager to win the honor of the prizes. At the ball many people keep their votes for themselves, try to steal other people's votes, and even attack the winners, the two people acknowledged to have the most beautiful costumes. In short, the crowd feels nothing but envy toward the winners and is incapable of either enjoying or admiring the beauty of the costumes. Like Peredonov, the townspeople wish only to destroy beauty.

Perhaps as an ironical commentary on the rejection of art by Peredonov and the people of the town, Sologub works into the texture of the novel parodies and travesties of some of the most famous works of nineteenth-century Russian literature. Thus although his characters dismiss art, Sologub reaffirms the importance of literature by having them unconsciously, and in debased form, live out literary themes. Pushkin is an important presence in the novel. The phrase *"melkii bes,"* the book's title, appears in *Evgenii Onegin* when Tatiana's mother describes Pykhtin, one of Tatiana's would-be suitors. Literally the line translates "How profuse he was, like a petty demon," an idiomatic usage which means, "How he fawned on her" (VII, 26, 6). Pykhtin's pursuit of Tatiana comes to nothing, as does Peredonov's pursuit of the eligible women in the town; he ends up with Varvara. Perhaps more to the point, Peredonov in the course of the novel fawns ever more desperately—and hopelessly—on the princess, even writing her a love letter, in the hopes of getting the inspector's job. Another reference to *Evgenii Onegin* can be found in Peredonov's murder of his closest friend and imaginary rival, Volodin, a broad parody of Onegin's needless slaughter of his friend, Lenskii. Pushkin is also invoked in the scene in which each Rutilov sister tells Peredonov what she will give him if he marries her—a parody of the beginning of "Skazka o tsare Saltane" ("The Tale of Tsar Saltan") in which three sisters say what they would do for the tsar if they became queen.[3] Dar'ia, like the first sister in Pushkin's tale, promises good cooking, but not in a very gracious way: "I will bake you the most delicious *bliny*—hot ones—only don't choke yourself on them." In contrast to the woven cloth promised by Pushkin's second sister, Liudmila promises to tell Peredonov all the gossip in the town. And whereas the third of Puhskin's heroines promises to give the king an heir, Valeriia is far more suggestive: "The whimsical, delicate face of Valeriia appeared a moment between the cheerful faces of her two sisters and her fragile little voice could be heard: 'And I wouldn't for anything tell you what I'll give you—guess for yourself!'" (85). There are other parallels with Pushkin's tale. Pushkin's tsar accidentally overhears the three sisters' offers as he rides past their window. In *The Petty Demon* Peredonov demands to know what the sisters will do for him but refuses Dar'ia's request that they be allowed to tell him from the window. Pushkin's tsar marries the youngest sister, but Peredonov decides against marrying Valeriia because she would not allow him to beat her, and then turns down the other two as well.

There are also echoes of Gogol's *Dead Souls* in the novel. Peredonov's visits to the prominent people in the town recall those of Chichikov in Gogol's novel, and Volodin's resemblance to a sheep brings to mind Sobakevich's likeness to a bear. On his wedding day Peredonov tries to get a "Spanish haircut," probably an allusion to Gogol's story "Zapiski sumasshedshego" ("Notes of a Madman"). Like Peredonov, Gogol's protagonist goes mad; he believes he is the king of Spain and that the mental hospital to which he is sent is Spain. He is therefore surprised that all the people have shaved heads. It may be, then, that by a Spanish haircut Peredonov means that he wishes to be shaved bald, possibly to distinguish himself from his curly-headed nemesis, Volodin.[4]

Echoes of Dostoevsky are also suggested by the rumor, scandal, and intrigue that shock the provincial town in *The Petty Demon*[5]. The ball and the fire in the finale of Sologub's novel decidedly bring to mind the finale of *The Possessed*, as does the novel's title. (In Russian *The Possessed* is called *Besy*, or *The Devils*.) These literary allusions make an important point. Although Peredonov's madness certainly does not constitute art, Sologub's brilliant use of patterning and literary allusion creates a novel of unquestionable artistic power.

I have tried to demonstrate in this chapter how Peredonov

generates the escalating pattern of events in the novel, how most of what happens to him can be directly or indirectly traced back to him. On the level of cause and effect or karma, he mistreats people who later exact their revenge; on an epistomological level, he confuses words, thoughts, and reality, then acts on his confusion with disastrous results; on the most basic, ontological level, he rejects any form of relationship with nature, religion, children, women and art—five ways of reaching out to others by reaching into one's self, and he perishes through lack of contact with the world.

I should add here that in rejecting various ways out of isolation, Peredonov, the petty demon, merely represents an extreme form of the spiritual sickness that afflicts his entire world. We have seen how the entire town rejects art. For creations of truth and beauty they substitute harmful, untrue creations in the form of gossip, slander and denunciations. If Peredonov fears nature, the other people in the town are merely oblivious to it. In their free time they generally stay indoors and indulge in obsessive card-playing, billiards and parties. Peredonov fears religion because he fears God, but the other characters (except for some of the children) are unaware of God; they go to services either to be socially acceptable (Volodin's motive) or to enjoy the smell of the incense and the elegance of the ritual (Liudmila's reason for going). Similarly, Peredonov expends a great deal of energy and ingenuity in tormenting children, but the latter are routinely beaten by their parents. And if Peredonov does not relate well to women it is clear that in the mad world in which he lives petty intrigues invariably substitute for meaningful relationships between people. Peredonov is the source and examplar of petty evil in his world. His breakdown shows us that the logical conclusion of destructiveness is self-destruction.

Chapter 7
Setting

Setting in the sense of the time and place in which the action of a novel occurs is straightforward in *The Petty Demon*. Sologub set the novel at the time he was writing it—at the end of the nineteenth century—and in a small town in the second district of Ruban Province, hardly unusual as there is a long tradition of satirical Russian novels set in the provinces. Pushkin satirized provincial society in *Evgenii Onegin*, as did Gogol in *Dead Souls* among other works; Dostoevsky did so in *The Possessed* and *The Brothers Karamazov* and so did Saltykov-Shchedrin in *The History of a Town, Provincial Sketches* and *The Golovlevs*. In all these works, as in *The Petty Demon*, the authors excoriated the small minds, dullness, boredom, mediocrity, pettiness, conventionality and often the corruption of provincial society. Most of these authors did not believe city life to be any better, but only more sophisticated in its corruption. This would appear to have been Sologub's opinion as well. Certainly, Peredonov's visit to Petersburg which he recounts in the first pages of the novel does not help him shake off his petty delusions, but only confirms them.

It is not in the setting *per se* but in Sologub's use of place and time that *The Petty Demon* is unique, as a comparison with realistic novels will demonstrate. In most realistic novels long and intense scenes occur in a fairly limited number of locations and these take on increasing meaning, symbolizing aspects of a character or even the character himself. For example, the *maison* Vauquer in the famous description at the beginning of *Le Père Goriot* epitomizes its owner and sets the scene both physically and emotionally for much of the action that follows.[1] Similarly, Oblomovka (Oblomov's childhood home in Goncharov's novel) holds the key to the protagonist's character as well as being a place he carries around inside himself for his entire life. Specific locations in realistic novels can also serve as a focus for events, the place where important things happen. The haymarket serves this function in *Crime and Punishment*; it is the crossroads of Raskol'nikov's part of the city, where he goes when he feels most desperate and where he is finally able to kiss the earth and so return to God and to human society. Trains play a similar role in *Anna Karenina*. Anna meets Vronsky in a train station, he courts her on a train and she finally commits suicide on a train track.

In the Sasha-Liudmila subplot Sologub uses Liudmila's room in such a traditionally realistic way. Her room is the focus of action in the subplot; Sasha and Liudmila first meet in Sasha's landlady's house and take walks together but gradually as the action becomes more erotic, it is increasingly restricted to Liudmila's room. The room is also symbolic of Liudmila herself; it is her sphere of influence, the symbol of her power and its source, the place where she experiences her erotic dreams and fantasies. It is here that she dresses Sasha in her clothes and introduces him to sensuality. At the end of the novel Sasha issues from it transformed into a Japanese geisha and able to lie convincingly to his landlady and aunt.

In the principal story line concerning Peredonov, however, Sologub's use of place differs markedly from that of realist novelists. Here action occurs in a number of locations with no one place dominant. Furthermore, unlike other nineteenth-century novels and the Sasha-Liudmila subplot, no significant contact between Peredonov and the other characters ever occurs and so there are never any long or intense scenes.

Since location is only as significant as the events that happen there, no location can be meaningful for Peredonov. He constantly moves from place to place as if he were looking for something, a searcher for some kind of comfort, answer, or escape from his life. We follow him as he makes regular stops at his apartment, Vershina's, the church, the headmaster's, the billiard parlor and occasional visits to Ademenko, Grushina's and the barber. He visits all the town officials and many of his students. Peredonov, however, does not bring to these changes of scene the change of orientation that would be necessary for him to reach out to others and feel better, and so for him all locations become more or less interchangeable. By the end of the novel he has lost the very concept of place—of physical extension in space—the difference between what exists and what does not, and his story takes on a very insubstantial quality.

Interestingly, the only house in the town Peredonov will not enter is Rutilov's. In Chapter 4 he insists on waiting outside even though he is choosing which Rutilov sister to marry. Peredonov's refusal to enter the Rutilov house maintains distance between the main story line and the Sasha-Liudmila subplot: Liudmila Rutilov's house is off limits to Peredonov. This also establishes a complementary relationship between Peredonov and Sasha, since Sasha spends a great deal of time at the Rutilov house and Peredonov will go anywhere but there. In linguistics, if two sound occur in mutually exclusive environments ("complimentary distribution"), they are considered two forms of the same phoneme. Although Sasha and Peredonov are obviously not the same person, their "complementary distribution" in reference to the Rutilovs' house emphasizes some of the parallels between them mentioned earlier. In staying outside the Rutilov sisters' house Peredonov rejects their eroticism and power. By spending time in Liudmila's room Sasha gives himself over to it. Between them they describe two equally undesirable extremes: Sasha is corrupted by eroticism and Peredonov is destroyed by a lack of love that expresses itself in a fear of women.

As in everything else, Peredonov's attitude toward place is true to a lesser degree of the rest of his town. Characters congregate at parties, billiard parlors, at each other's houses but although each of these locations is described in detail, none of them has any significance. The reader realizes that the various houses in the town, like the rest of the characters' lives, represent only clutter—attempts on the part of the characters to fill the spiritual void of their lives with meaningless social interactions within meaningless locations.

The second component of setting is time. With the exception of Sterne's *Tristram Shandy* in which the reader's time is compared to the writer's time and the characters' time, authors of nineteenth-century novels did not ostentatiously manipulate the actual flow of time itself. This is not to deny that authors heighten tension by compressing many events into a short period of time (as, for example, in *Crime and Punishment*), or expand and universalize a story by expanding it over many years (*War and Peace*), or change the order of events through flashbacks and flash forwards (e.g., *A Hero of Our Time*). In all these novels, however, time seems to flow at an even rate and only the density or order of events changes.

In *The Petty Demon* the flow of time itself seems fitful and sometimes absent. It is difficult to see how the actual events of the novel could happen in less than two months. In the course of the novel Peredonov visits Marta's family in the country, Peredonov and Varvara move, Peredonov spends a week visiting officials, an undisclosed amount of time visiting students, instigates a plot to tar Marta's gate which involves four people (Peredonov tells Volodin to do it, Volodin tells Cherepnin, Cherepnin gets the locksmith's sons to do it), Peredonov tries to marry off Volodin, Peredonov and Varvara marry and wait a week and a half for the headmaster to visit them, Peredonov writes many denunciations, one a night, goes to a masquerade ball, starts getting anonymous letters about Varvara's trick and finally kills Volodin. Yet all indications of the passage of time (weather, seasons, days of the week, sequential narration) seem to be defective or lacking. The effect is to make the reader feel that the novel is taking place in a timeless hell, an impression that grows throughout the novel.

In the course of the novel we do not get a sense that the weather has generally gotten colder as it would, for example, between September and November. Instead, there is a kind of eternal autumn. The weather gets hot and cool, wet and dry arbitrarily. In the first chapter when Peredonov visits Vershina, flowers and fruit are blooming in her garden. In Chapter 6 it is still warm enough for Vladia to go barefoot. The weather is described as gloomy in Chapters 8 and 9, cold, windy and with long cold rains in Chapter 14. There is a fine rain in Chapter 18, and in Chapter 19 Marta and Vershina have moved inside and Peredonov is wearing a coat. Yet in Chapter 21 the day is extremely clear and hot and Marta is knitting in the summer house. In Chapter 22 there is rain again, yet in Chapter 24 it is warm enough for Peredonov and Volodin to sit in the park. In Chapter 26 the air is warm and Sasha and Liudmila go to a ravine to be cool, while Chapter 32 again describes a cold, bleak day. The changes in the weather seem to reflect the characters' moods or author's convenience much more than they do the progression of the seasons. The effect of these capricious changes in the weather is to disorient the reader in time. There is no relationship between weather and season, and the town seems to exist on its own separate plane, "alienated from heaven."

Sologub also creates a feeling of timelessness by alternating great specificity of time with great vagueness. The first three chapters of the novel preserve perfect continuity of time. We follow Peredonov around for the entire day. Suddenly in Chapter 4 Peredonov is playing billiards and we have no idea how much time has elapsed. Chapters 6-12 recount with great accuracy Peredonov's actions on every day of the week from Saturday to the following Sunday. Yet in Chapter 12 the time sequence breaks down again. We are told, "On the next day Peredonov and Varvara finally moved." That "next day" cannot be Monday, as it should be, because Peredonov does not go to the *gimnaziia* to teach, but instead spends the day cutting up Varvara's dress and playing billiards. We are again out of time. In Chapters 16 and 17 continuity of time is again briefly reinstated. And while in Chapter 21 we learn it is Sunday, and Peredonov's wedding in Chapter 23 is on a Wednesday, these are only isolated identifiable points in a fog of timelessness. Much more often, and increasingly toward the end of the novel, the narrator uses terms such as "one day," "the next day," "that evening," "once," "early in the morning," which give a timeless or fairy tale feeling to events and reflect Peredonov's growing disorientation.

Sologub most effectively creates a feeling of timelessness, however, by his increasing use of verbs in the imperfective aspect. In Russian the imperfective aspect expresses a repeated action or process, while the perfective aspect expresses a one-time or completed action. In *The Petty Demon* one-time (perfective) actions, which imply change, increasingly cede to habitual (imperfective) actions which describe the eternal futility of the characters' lives. Thus the passage of time becomes irrelevant:

> Each time as Peredonov went past (*prokhodil*) Vershina's garden, Vershina stopped (*ostanavlivala*) him and with her prophetic words and gestures lured (*zamanivala*) him into the garden (111).

> As usual, Vershina lured (*zamanivala*) him with her prophetic calls, as usual Rutilov praised (*vykhvalial*) his sisters. At home Varvara urged (*ugovarivala*) him to marry her quickly—but he couldn't reach any decision (*nikakogo resheniia ne prinimal on*) (150).

> Each day he visited (*poseshchal*) another student's house (150).

> Volodin faithfully went (*khodil*) to the Adamenkos to give lessons (213).

> Peredonov's eccentric behavior worried (*bespokoil*)

Khripach [the director of the *gimnaziia*] more and more
each day (261).

Sometimes Peredonov protected himself with magic
spells (*churalsia*) from the cat (323).

From time to time Prepolovenskaia sent (*posylala*)
anonymous letters to Peredonov (333).

Time passed but the document appointing him
inspector, anticipated from day to day, did not arrive
(*prikhodila*) (334).

Every day he composed (*sostavlial*) a denunciation of his
enemies (340).

Sometimes Peredonov took (*bral*) some playing cards
and with a furious expression chopped (*raskalyval*) the
heads off the court cards with a penknife (343).

The increase in frequency of these "imperfectivizing" statements
toward the end of the novel mirrors Peredonov's fading grasp of
events and the feeling that he is on a treadmill. These statements
powerfuly contribute to the crescendo pattern of madness in the
novel.

Setting, the flow of time and the significance of place, in a
novel is usually a background aspect because we take it for granted
as we do such things as the force of gravity or sanity itself. When
the setting seems peculiar, however, as in *The Petty Demon*, it
assumes a primary, foreground importance. Here it disturbs the
reader on two counts. First, the peculiarities of time and space in
the novel make it impossible to plant ourselves securely in this
world. Just as Sologub does not allow us to identify with
characters or lose ourselves in the plot, so he does not create a
solid, three-dimensional world for us, but one that is on the brink
of dissolution. For readers used to entering realistic novelistic
worlds without thinking, this is subliminally, but all the more
powerfully disconcerting.

Secondly, and more seriously, orientation in time and space is
basic to our sense of control and reality. As Peredonov's
awareness of time and space attenuates and eventually disappears,
we, too, are made to experience this loss through devices such as
the repeated use of imperfective verbs, or the lack of the
progression of the seasons. This is profoundly disturbing but since
we are not used to looking at setting carefully, we cannot find the

source of our discomfort and thus cannot express it except in vague irritation at Sologub.

Although the critics did not comment on Sologub's use of time and space in *The Petty Demon*, I suspect that the empty places and fitful time flow made them feel uncomfortable without quite knowing why. Perhaps their personal attacks on Sologub in part represented an expression of this frustration.

Chapter 8
Narration

Although every novel, as an "extended prose narrative" (and as opposed to a play, for example) must have a narrator, this basic constituent by its very nature is difficult to discuss. Since in most novels the author directs our attention to the characters and plot, we tend to dismiss the narrator—the medium through whom we learn the story—in the same way we dismiss the window pane through which we see the street. In order to look for warps in the glass, or in the narrator, we must make an effort to refocus our attention. Such an effort is particularly important for an understanding of *The Petty Demon* in which I believe the narrator to be the most significant and overlooked element. Like character, plot, and setting, narration in *The Petty Demon* is neither realistic nor modernist. Its uniqueness is best seen against some of the universals of narration which apply to *The Petty Demon* as well.

The narrator of any novel occupies a no man's land between the fictional world he describes and the "real" world. On the one hand he mediates between the reader and the characters, explaining their actions and motivations to us; on the other hand he mediates between the author and the characters, acting as the author's representative, sometimes reflecting the author's values but in no way identical with the author.[1] The narrator can fulfill his first role—to mediate between the characters and the reader—because he exists on a different level from the characters. Whereas the characters must go through time to know the future, the narrator (even a first-person narrator) already knows the outcome of the characters' actions. The narrator is not only free from time but can control time and the reader's perception of events, as mentioned above, through flashbacks, flash forwards, compression, acceleration or slowing down the narration of events. The first time he reads a novel the reader is in the same position as the characters, not knowing the outcome of events, or the significance of actions for the future. In subsequent readings, however, th⸢ reader joins the narrator in his awareness of events out of ⸜⸍

and, knowing the outcome of the novel, is able to enjoy the work in a less suspense-filled, but more aesthetic and dispassionate way.

In *The Petty Demon* the endless and seemingly random events that barrage the first-time reader who wants to find out what happens next, begin to assume a shape the second time he reads the novel. The early impression of chaotic events subsides and the reader can concern himself with larger issues. He begins to see how Peredonov's actions and thoughts contribute to a pattern, that there are parallels between Peredonov and his friends, and that the novel is funny in a previously unsuspected way.

For example, when Peredonov visits the prosecutor, he is greeted angrily: "'Have you come to turn yourself in? Did you kill someone? Did you set a fire? Did you rob the post office?' Avinovitskii yelled angrily, admitting Peredonov into the drawing room, 'or have you yourself been the victim of a crime, which is more than possible in our town'" (143).

The reader who is familiar with the novel is aware that by the end of it Peredonov will have killed Volodin, set fire to the community hall and been victimized by forged letters. Peredonov is terrified of the prosecutor and perceives him as a punitive authority figure who can guess his transgressions even before he commits them. The prosecutor's seeming prescience of the outcome of the novel gives a realistic basis for Peredonov's childish fear of him.

Many early critics of *The Petty Demon* chose to ignore the narrator's second role: to mediate between author and characters. Their outrage at Peredonov's pettiness and sadism led them not only to ignore the narrator, but to identify author with protagonist. Hence the claims that Sologub was, in fact, Peredonov.[2] Some idea of the prevalence of these attacks can be gained from the fact that Sologub felt it necessary to insist in the preface to the second edition of the novel that he was not Peredonov: "I was not forced by necessity to compose and make things up from within myself," he wrote. "Everything that is anecdotal, psychological or a slice of life in my novel is based on very precise observations and I had sufficient models for my novel all around me . . . . No, my dear contemporaries, it is about you I wrote my novel . . . about you" (32).

In *The Petty Demon* the distinctions among protagonist, narrator and author are clear enough. The narrator, who is not crazy, tells us about Peredonov, who is. Behind the narrator stands Sologub. Although the latter, like Peredonov, served as a provincial *gimnaziia* teacher for many years, unlike him, he did become a school inspector and did not go crazy. He is also greater than the narrator in that he has integrated his experience sufficiently, summoned enough objectivity and is gifted with enough skill to create a novel. Nonetheless, we cannot attribute the critics' confusion of Sologub with Peredonov simply to their discomfort with the novel. There is, in fact, someting peculiar in the way the narrator mediates between author and characters, a peculiarity which can best be seen in relation to narrators in general.

Because narrators exist on a plane between the characters and the author, they tend to resemble one or the other to varying degrees. Thus, it is possible to distinguish between "character" narrators and "authorial" narrators. Character narrators draw attention to themselves and speak to us in a distinctive voice. The narrator of *The Brothers Karamazov*, for example, talks about "our town" and the narrator of *The Possessed* actually takes part in the action of the novel. Henry James's rigorously limited first person narrators fall within this group, as, of course does Conrad's favorite narrator, Marlowe.[3] The narrator of *The Petty Demon* differs from these. From the first paragraph of the novel he talks about "this town," not "our town," never reveals anything about himself and talks of the characters' feelings and actions with unselfconscious and complete authority. This narrator is on the same educational and intellectual level as the reader, generally not the case with "character" narrators (e.g., the narrator of Gogol's "How Ivan Ivanovich Quarrelled with Ivan Nikiforovich"), and unlike "character" narrators, who judge characters as good or bad, wise or foolish, the narrator of *The Petty Demon* rarely voices his opinion. Instead, he usually gives us the facts of the characters' thoughts and actions and leaves the reader to make his own judgments. This is a very effective device as the reader reacts in spontaneous distaste to Peredonov and others without the narrator's coaching. The scene in Chapter 18 in which Peredonov and Iuliia Gudaevskaia try to beat Antosha while Nikolai tries to stop them, for example, is even more horrifying because the narrator recounts the events in a matter-of-fact manner, without comment.

But although the narrator of *The Petty Demon* is not a "character" narrator, he also differs from the "authorial" type closely associated with realism—the omniscient self-effacing, almost invisible narrators typical of Turgenev, Flaubert or Tolstoy. From a technical point of view *The Petty Demon* could not have such a narrator because in a story about illusion told primarily from the point of view of a character going mad, the reader must be made aware of the difference between what Peredonov thinks he is seeing, hearing and feeling, and what, in fact, is actually happening. Thus from time to time the narrator must make himself visible to explain events to us. In Chapter 12, for example, when Peredonov goes to church he is disturbed by the disorderliness of the students. At this point the narrator intervenes to tell us the actual state of affairs: "In fact, the students stood decorously and modestly. Some crossed themselves unconsciously, thinking about something other than church, others prayed diligently. Very rarely someone whispered something to his neighbor . . . . But these small movements unnoticed by the class monitors produced an illusion of great disorder in Peredonov's disturbed but dull sensibilities" (177).

The narrator of *The Petty Demon* also intervenes to tell us when other characters perceive things incorrectly. For example, Vershina is convinced that Peredonov is in love with Marta at the beginning of the novel, but this, the narrator lets us know, is not true. Varvara mistakenly thinks that Peredonov's strange behavior is due to drinking.

More important than these technical interventions, however, are the narrator's occasional but passionate comments on the action which draw our attention to him and distinguish him from his invisible, realistic counterpart. There are several digresssions on what he calls "the profaning of beauty." He regrets, for example, that Varvara and Grushina corrupt the beauty of their bodies in the passages quoted above (p. 86). He is even more passionate in his digression about Dar'ia whose drunken caterwauling profanes the beauty of the Russian folk song she sings:

> Oh fatal anguish resounding in the fields and villages of our broad native expanses! An anguish embodied in wild clamoring, anguish which like a vile flame, devours the living word, reducing once living song to mindless howling. O fatal anguish, o dear, old Russian song, will you really die? (210)

Here Dar'ia's singing is generalized to represent an attack by the petty and miserable Russian people on the spirit of Russia. Dar'ia, like all Russians, the narrator tells us, is filled with Peredonovism. That is, she expresses her unhappiness by transforming living beauty into ugliness and death.

Although the narrator generally presents Peredonov's thoughts and actions without comment, there is an important series of digressions in which he expresses compassion for Peredonov and even tries to influence the reader to feel compassion. It may be that Sologub felt that Peredonov would be too monstrous without occasional interpretation by the narrator. These digressions are important because they confer significance on Peredonov and suggest parallels between him and us. In one digression the narrator describes the unhappiness of the town and of Peredonov: "Amidst the weariness on the streets and in the houses, under this alienation from heaven, on an impure, impotent earth walked Peredonov and he was tormented by vague fears—and there was no consolation for him from above and no joy on earth because now, as always, he looked at the world through dead eyes, like some demon, tormented in dismal loneliness by terror and ennui" (141). There are further digressions, discussed above, which concern Peredonov's fear and hatred of religion and nature and in which the narrator points out that Peredonov would suffer less if he could accept either of these outlets to feel connected with something. Toward the end, the narrator links Peredonov's insanity to a search for a higher truth: "His mad, dull eyes wandered and didn't fix on things, as if he always wanted to look beyond them, to the other side of the material world, and he was searching for apertures of some kind" (366). The effect of these digressions is to exalt Peredonov, the ludicrous, sadistic, crazy teacher, to a symbol of man's unsuccessful search for higher truth and unity with the cosmos.

Even further from realism than the narrator's occasional digressions explaining Peredonov to the reader, is a certain half-humorous sympathy with Peredonov's deranged view of his world. We have described how Peredonov's fear of the town prosecutor is validated. Another example of such validation is the narrator's agreement with Peredonov concerning Volodin's resemblance to a sheep. Despite Volodin's conformist attitude, his stupidity, his willingness to be led by Peredonov in everything, and the dream he recounts in Chapter 22 in which he is made king of the sheep in heaven (or perhaps the Lamb of God), no other character in the novel besides Peredonov comments on the similarity. Peredonov, of course, believes that Volodin is literally a sheep, but as if in sympathy, the narrator describes Volodin as a sheep on his first appearance, frequently uses "bleated" instead of "said" when Volodin speaks, and often describes him as butting with his head, and sticking out his lips in an offended manner.

Similarly, Peredonov's perception of women as witches is echoed by the narrator, although, as in the case of Volodin, on a metaphorical, not on a literal level:

Vershina would stop him and with her prophetic gestures and words would lure him into the garden.

He entered, involuntarily surrendering to her gentle sorcery (111).

The [Rutilov] sisters were young and beautiful and their voices rang out clear and wild—the witches on Bald Mountain would have envied them their round dance (211).

The narrator's partial agreement with Peredonov's view of things indicates that in some way Peredonov sees further than his half-dead neighbors. Such keener vision, however, does Peredonov no good since everything passes through the distorting lens of his insanity and thus is transformed into terrifying halluciations.

The strange and complex narrator who, while clearly not a character, sympathizes partially with the protagonist's delusions may have confused some critics and led them to identify Sologub with Peredonov. But if we go further and consider the uncanny and confusing effect such a non-realistic narrator has on us, we will be led into the heart of the novel. I believe that the source of the disturbing power of *The Petty Demon* lies in the fact that Sologub through the narrator induces in us, the reader, for the duration of the novel, a state of disorientation equivalent to Peredonov's; in reading this novel about a breakdown we experience a parallel sense of helplessness, loss of control and unreality.

This may seem a difficult proposition to accept. But we have already seen how Sologub dislocates our sense of time and space along with Peredonov's as the novel progresses. More subtle, yet even more powerful than the setting, I believe, are the peculiarities of the narration and the vague doubts they raise in us. Like Peredonov, we experience an agonizing conflict between trust and mistrust, a fear of not being able to tell friends from enemies; our doubts, however, are in relation to the narrator.

To produce such a state in a reader is no easy matter. Sologub succeeds because his narrator presents us with two aspects. On the surface he is a trustworthy guide to the underworld; he explains what is "really" happening, he interprets Peredonov's thoughts for us when necessary, he reassures us that he, like us, disapproves of the profanation of beauty. In a world so far removed from our own we experience the narrator's extra involvement (extra, that is, by realistic standards) both as necessary and comforting.

We scarcely notice the narrator's second, darker aspect: conveyor to the underworld. Gradually, without our even realizing it, but from the very beginning, he first disorients us and then leads us to accept Peredonov's disturbed way of thinking. We can see this process clearly if we compare the way realistic novels begin with the beginning of *The Petty Demon*. Usually, in realistic novels, the first sentence takes us into the story, either by describing the protagonist or by sounding a theme that will dominate the novel, or by describing a location in which major events will take place, as in the following examples:

Le Père Goriot: Madame Vauquer, whose maiden name was de Conflans, was an old woman who, for forty years had run a middle-class rooming house on the rue Neuve-Sainte-Genevière, between the Latin Quarter and the suburb of Saint-Marceau.

Crime and Punishment: At the beginning of July, in the extremely hot time toward evening, a certain young man left his garret which he rented from the tenants in S. lane and slowly, as if in indecision, set off for the K-n bridge.

War and Peace: "Well, prince, Genoa and Lucca are just appanages, estates of the Bonapart family."

Oblomov: In Gorokhovy Street, in one of those large houses whose population is that of an entire district center, Il'ia Il'ich Oblomov lay in the morning, in his apartment, in bed.

Fathers and Sons: "Well, Peter, can't you see them yet?" asked a gentleman on May 20, 1859, going out without his hat on the narrow porch of the inn on -

Street, a gentleman of about 40-odd, with dusty coat
and checked trousers who addressed his servant, a
young and plump chap with whitish down on his chin
and little dull eyes.

Even modernists start their novels this way, although the intention
is sometimes tongue-in-cheek:

Petersburg: Apollon Apollonovich Ableukhov was of
estimable stock: he had Adam for an ancestor.

The Master and Margarita: One day in the spring
during a fantastically warm summer, in Moscow at
Patriarch's Pond two citizens appeared.

The Hamlet: A little while before sundown the men
lounging about the gallery of the store saw, coming up
the road from the south, a covered wagon drawn by
mules and followed by a considerable string of obviously
alive objects which in the leveling sun resembled
varisized and -colored tatters torn at random from large
billboards—circus posters, say—attached to the rear of
the wagon and inherent with its own separate and
collective motion, like the tail of a kite.

Women in Love: Ursula and Gudrun Brangwen sat one
morning in the window-bay of their father's house in
Beldover, working and talking.

The Petty Demon begins as follows:

Mass was over and the parishioners were dispersing to
their homes.   Some were lingering in the gateway
behind the white stone walls, under the old lindens and
maples and conversing.   Everyone was dressed in their
Sunday best, regarded one another politely, and it
seemed that in this town people lived together
peacefully and amiably.   And even happily.   But all
this only seemed.[4]

In contrast to the above examples, the first sentence does not
pique our curiosity; what could be less startling than parishioners
going home after mass?   Nor does it introduce us to the novel's
protagonist.   Indeed, the word "parishioner" seems inapplicable to
any of the petty, spiteful characters we later meet in the novel.
Nor does the first sentence sound a central theme or describe an
important location.   Religion in general and the town church in

particular, as we have seen, do play a role in the novel, but hardly the major one.

The paragraph as a whole, however, could be said to create an important and recurring mood in the reader: a feeling of disorientation. The narrator has presented us with a conventional and even staid picture of small-town stability, complete with church service, maple trees and friendly people—and then immediately told us that it is false. In so doing he has warned us that things in this novel may not be the way they seem. But because we have only the narrator to tell us about the world of the novel, we find ourselves from the very beginning confused and uneasily awaiting the next jolt. This sense of disorientation grows in us as we read the narrator's calm descriptions of the characters' strange and cruel actions, as, for example when Peredonov spits on Varvara. What kind of world is this, we wonder.

But beyond disorienting us, the narrator, as conveyor to the underworld, leads us to accept Peredonov's disturbed way of thinking. Peredonov's thought is characterized by the fact that he imposes his private patterns (discussed in Chapter 6) on reality. Thus, for example, when he sees Varvara reading a cookbook, his belief that she is a witch and hostile to him leads him to conclude that she either wants to bewitch or poison him. Peredonov never checks his assumptions to see if they are valid or even meaningful. Something similar happens to us as we read the novel. We, too, start to accept arbitrary patterns without questioning them. Like Peredonov we begin to find the pattern more significant than its meaning. At the beginning of the novel, for example, it is difficult to understand Peredonov's attractiveness to women, especially since the narrator repeatedly describes him as "gloomy," "spiteful," "uninterested in anything that does not concern him personally," and as having a "convulsive laugh." Yet, as we see the many women who are willing and even eager to marry him—Varvara, Marta, the Rutilov sisters, Prepolovenskaia's niece—we somehow accept Peredonov's attractiveness to women. Further, Varvara's fear that Peredonov might run off in the middle of the night and marry someone in order to throw her out of his apartment seems ridiculous out of the context of the novel. Surely, no man would get married on impulse in the middle of the night just to humiliate and get rid of an unwanted mistress, and surely no woman would want a man whose principal and announced motive for getting married was to spite another woman. But when

Rutilov drags Peredonov off one evening to choose and marry on
the spot one of his sisters, and when all three women seem willing
to undergo humiliation for the chance of becoming Peredonov's
wife, we begin to accept Varvara's fears as natural. They are part
of a pattern.

We accept the party at Peredonov's apartment in which the
main entertainment consists of ripping the wallpaper off the walls;
we accept Peredonov's mechanical drunken dance with Ershova
around the pear tree; Varvara's unlikely scheme to forge letters
from the Princess, and its success; Volodin's fatuous anticipation
that Nadezhda Adamenko, who is well educated and wealthy will
marry him. We accept without even realizing it the peculiar
language, logic, and motivation of this world which the narrator
presents to us as a whole and with authority, no longer aware that
we would dismiss as meaningless any one incident, character of
conversation if encountered in isolation. As conveyor to the
underworld the narrator casts a spell over us similar to the one
Peredonov feels has been cast over him.

This is not to identify madness with art or the reader with
Peredonov. Of course our experience with the novel is very
different from Peredonov's because we read the novel voluntarily
and with perspective. Patterning, however, can be used in the
service of either art or madness. I believe the narrator of this
novel—through event-patterning (as we have seen in Chapter Six)
and through catching us up in the illogical but consistent patterns
governing the characters' motivation and behavior—attempts to
create an aesthetic equivalent of madness in the reader for the
duration of the novel.

This aesthetic equivalent of Peredonov's madness, however,
does not entirely overwhelm us. Somewhere we know that
something is wrong, but we do not know what. And so, while we
do not question the motives and actions of the characters, we resist
the novel as a whole. The problem is our inability to see how the
narrator contributes to our confusion. The barely conscious conflict
in our feelings toward the narrator who is both guide and seducer
leaves us with a tremendous sense of confusion and irritation about
the novel. Like Peredonov, but with better cause, we both want
to trust, but do not dare.

Trust between reader and narrator is the glue of realistic
fiction. Without trust there can be no "fiction of a shared
reality." Douglas Hewitt believes that even the description of

characters provided by realistic narrators are more important as a means of establishing the reader's confidence in the narrator than as a source of specific information:

> We do not say "these data add up to a coherent picture of a young woman" but "I trust this writer [George Eliot, for example] to tell me the truth and I accept these tidbits as what she wishes for the moment to comment on in the character of a person whom I accept on her word." . . . Realistic novels do not affect us as being lifelike; they are like the experience of being told about life by someone we trust.[5]

While untrustworthy narrators often appear in modern novels (in the works of Henry James and Vladimir Nabokov, for example) these are generally first person "character" narrators, unlike the one in *The Petty Demon*. The disturbing, mind-bending quality of this novel consists in the following: Sologub gives the narrator realistic mannerisms—the narrator introduces us to each character, maintains a third-person, seemingly objective view of events and assumes an alliance with the reader—but the world the narrator shows us is disintegrating in a most unrealistic way. We are confused by this dissonance between the tone of the narration and the events of the novel, and thus we are more vulnerable to Sologub's insidious intention: slowly but inexorably to recreate in us Peredonov's spiritual dilemma. This is an exceedingly unpleasant process for us to experience. We are only consoled, the novel is only redeemed, by the dazzling artistry of its execution.

Chapter 9
The Petty Demon and Symbolism

I began this study of *The Petty Demon* by connecting the novel's originality and power with the political and literary climate that gave rise to the Russian symbolist movement. Having examined its unique form, I would like, before concluding, to consider the novel against the later development of symbolism. After all, in the seventeen years between the time Sologub started work on *The Petty Demon* and its first complete publication, symbolism had become the most prestigious literary trend of its day, and Sologub one of its well-known practitioners. The questions arise, then, To what extent is *The Petty Demon* a "symbolist novel" and what, exactly, does it owe to the symbolist movement?

Russian symbolism, which arose around 1890 and started to decline around 1910, is most commonly divided into two periods or "generations": up to 1904 or 1905 the movement is said to have been led by the aesthetic or decadent French or Belgian wing, typified in the poetry of Valerii Briusov and Konstantin Bal'mont; after 1905 the religious or metaphysical German wing led by Andrei Bely and Aleksandr Blok is said to have come to the fore. I am not convinced, however, of the usefulness of this two-generational scheme in understanding Sologub. First, Sologub's critics seem to have had trouble deciding whether Sologub (who along with most symbolists spanned both periods) should be classified as a decadent or a symbolist; he has been called both a member of the second "metaphysical" generation and "the only pure Russian decadent."[1]   Secondly, the generational theory of symbolism does not account for the fact that *The Petty Demon*—written in the first "decadent" period but published in the second "metaphysical" stage—was quite successful in the "wrong" period.   Finally, as I will show, Sologub's later work, his trilogy, *Tvorimaia legenda* (*A Legend in Creation*, 1907-1914), for example, is far more decadent than the earlier *Petty Demon*.

This is not to deny that 1905 marked a year of change for most aspects of Russian culture, including symbolism, but only to suggest that these changes can most easily be understood in terms of politics. In this year Russia lost the Russo-Japanese War, an unexpected and humiliating upset for a country that still remembered centuries of Mongolian rule. Apocalyptic and anti-Oriental themes quickly became popular among the symbolists.[2] Also in this year the liberal revolution—supported to some extent by much of the intelligentsia—failed, and as a result the revolutionary initiative shifted to more politically radical groups. Many liberals began to feel themselves equally alienated from the government and the revolutionary movement and withdrew from politics altogether. Russian symbolism also turned inward toward theoretical issues, and, in the case of Sologub, toward decadence.

The complex relationship between decadence and symbolism was integral to the symbolist movement. In France, decadence preceded symbolism by a few years and was partially incorporated into it. However, early Russian symbolists brought both movements into Russia together, along with what Kenneth Cornell refers to as the "long-drawn quarrel between the decadents and the symbolists, rather futile and none too clear." Briusov himself, who, as already mentioned, played a large part in bringing symbolism to Russia, used the terms "symbolism" and "decadence" interchangeably, but many Russian critics were at great pains to define the difference between the two, often with confusing results.[3]

Eventually, symbolism came to refer both to the new literature itself and to its dualistic philosophical underpinnings (discussed in Chapter One) which were developed in the course of the movement. Decadence, generally used as a pejorative term, came to refer to the escapist themes inherited from Baudelaire: a feeling of pessimism, and ennui about the world, solipsism, death, mystical love of evil, revolt against nature and love of the exotic.[4] As we have seen, contemporary critics attacked *The Petty Demon* along with its author as decadent, and more recent Soviet critics have followed suit. But is the novel in fact decadent?

We can take as a standard for comparison J. K. Huysmans' novel *A Rebours* (*Against the Grain*) which has been said to define the decadent spirit.[5] Written in 1884, the novel became a virtual manual for decadents. It concerns a rich young man, Duc Jean Floressas des Esseintes, the last descendant of a noble family, who withdraws from society into a totally isolated self-sufficient and self-created paradise/hell of the senses. Des Esseintes exalts the artistic and artificial and despises the natural. In his retreat he is surrounded by beautiful pictures and books, fine liqueurs and foods, jewels, exotic flowers and perfumes. Eventually des Esseintes' body and nerves rebel against this artificial existence and after a fitting finale in which he is forced to ingest food rectally to keep from starving to death, he rejoins the world, still unreconciled to it.

Here are all the elements of decadence: des Esseintes' desire to live alone in a self-created world of dreams and the senses is certainly solipsistic. Pessimism, indeed despair, is evident in the prayer which closes the novel: "Lord, take pity on the Christian who doubts, on the believer who would like to believe, on life's convict who embarks alone in the night, under a sky which the consoling beacons of the old hope no longer illumine!"[6] A mystical love of evil can be seen in des Esseintes' fascination with the relationship between sadism, which he feels is a direct outgrowth of Catholicism, and the black mass (Chapter 12). He is also fascinated by the pictures of Moreau and Goya, and by the writings of Poe and Baudelaire. His entire way of life is a revolt against nature and it almost destroys his body; his interest in exoticism takes the form of a love for writings from the time of the breakdown of the Roman Empire, another decadent era. Although des Esseintes' final inability to live *à rebours* might seem to argue against this being a decadent work, what is significant is that decadence here is presented as an extremely attractive ideal toward which man strives, even if unsuccessfully.

In contrast to Huysmans, Sologub in *The Petty Demon* presents all these themes negatively. For example, while des Esseintes' passion for the exotic is a sign of his superior taste, Liudmila's love for exotic perfumes and clothing is presented as tainted when she sprays Sasha with scent to brand him as hers, or dresses him in her clothes. When she dreams that Sasha is a snake or that he is being whipped, her mystical love of evil is not seen as romantic, but as an indication of her ties with Peredonov's pettiness and cruelty. Other decadent themes appear as symptoms of Peredonov's disease: his solipsistic belief that he is alone in the universe and that no one can help him is a reflection of his inability to extend himself to others; his revolt against nature in his cruelty to animals is far from being a noble ideal; his pessimism and ennui are measures of his blindness to the Dionysian ecstasies that the narrator tells us are all around him.

Sologub in fact did not endorse decadence in *The Petty Demon* written during the "decadent" stage of Russian symbolism. Between 1907 and 1914, however, when metaphysical symbolism is supposed to have been the order of the day, he wrote *A Legend in Creation*, a trilogy which in dramatic contrast to *The Petty Demon* shows decadence in a positive light.   The protagonist is Georgii Trirodov, a poet and alchemist who, although he shares several of Peredonov's characteristics, is presented as a positive, almost super-human character.   His ennui and pessimism are depicted as signs of his superiority; his revolt against nature in his desire to "kill the beast" (i.e., overcome human sexuality) presented as a noble ideal; the fact that he spends most of his time solipsistically day-dreaming in his study shows that he is a true artist.   Queen Ortruda, another major character in the novel who engages in murder, beatings and sadistic religious ceremonies is also presented sympathetically.   Escapism, so central to decadence, dominates this novel.   Indeed, escape from life, whether through fantasy, art or passion, is held to be life's goal.

It is logical to consider Sologub's disappointment at the failure of the 1905 revolution as at least one factor in the difference between the two novels.   *A Legend in Creation* is set during that revolution, concerns revolutionary activity, and ends in an apocalyptic fire in which most of the liberals are killed.   Before the fire Trirodov watches the liberals arguing with each other and sadly thinks, "Nothing for you will come to anything."   He pictures the liberals thrown into a deep abyss and perishing without descendants in the general destruction which he believes is coming.[7]   In this novel Sologub expressed his disillusionment with politics and society in general and concluded that for the artist withdrawal is the only alternative.

The influence of dualistic symbolist metaphysics on *The Petty Demon* is just as subtle as that of decadence.   At first glance Peredonov's grotesque world seems to be a lower sphere of existence than our own, and the narrator, who is on a higher level (as he demonstrates by his occasional criticisms and interpretations of it), seems to be showing us Peredonov's unsuccessful attempt to transcend his sordid reality and enter our world.   But this interpretation, although it flatters our vanity by putting us on the same superior level as the narrator, is not the whole story.   We,

along with Peredonov, as Sologub assures us in his preface, are the
subject of the novel, and on more than one occasion the narrator
draws parallels between Peredonov's world and ours.   When
Volodin refuses to wear a costume to the masquerade, for example,
and then envies those with costumes, the narrator includes us in
his comment: "Like many people, he was thoughtlessly and
spontaneously envious—after all, he himself was not wearing a
costume, so what was there to envy?" (391).   Similarly, we are
included in the narrator's description of Peredonov's problem:

> Blinded by the delusions of personality and of
> individual existence, he [Peredonov] didn't understand
> the elemental, Dionysian ecstasies rejoicing and crying in
> nature.   He was blind and pathetic like many of us.
> (311)

Peredonov, then, is the symbol—the eternal, general truth—of the
petty evil in our everyday selves.   The narrator, following
symbolist theory, both plunges us into Peredonov's world, and
allows us to glimpse something beyond it.   In this way he fulfills
the   role   of   the   symbolist   artist-priest,   enabling   his
audience-communicants to experience a brief transcendence.

Is *The Petty Demon*, then, a symbolist novel?   There is a
great deal of controversy over whether such a subgenre can be said
to exist.   Anna Balakian writes that a symbolist novel would be a
contradiction in terms since symbolists sought to evoke moods and
feelings, not to tell stories.[8]   But while many symbolists chose to
express themselves in short forms, I do not believe that long forms
were any less effective as a symbolist vehicle.   The great symbolist
novels—including *The Petty Demon*—by no means merely "told
stories," but applied symbolist principles to the novel genre.   Other
critics arguing for the symbolist novel as a subgenre characterize it
by the expanded role of the narrator.[9]   It is, indeed, characteristic
of the symbolists who believed in the power of the artist to
mediate between worlds, to exalt in novels the role of the narrator
who mediates among author, characters and reader.   As the artist
can momentarily unite this world with a higher one in his art, so
the narrator of the novel endeavors to unite the audience with the
author's created world.

However, it is not only the greater role of the narrator which,
in my opinion, distinguishes a symbolist novel, but the quality of
closeness among author, narrator, and protagonist.   Dostoevsky is

not Raskol'nikov, Flaubert is not Mme Bovary (despite his claim to the contrary) in the same way and with same intimacy that Huysmans is des Esseintes in *A Rebours*, Bely is Nikolai Apollonovich in *Petersburg*, d'Annunzio is George in *The Triumph of Death*.   The realistic balance among author, narrator, protagonist, and reader is shifted.   Instead of sharing an imaginary world with the author and narrator, as we do in realistic novels, the reader of a symbolist novel is in the position of being an outsider, perhaps even an intruder on the perfect understanding between the author-narrator and his creation.[10]   The advantage of such novels is that they present the writer with an opportunity to create a powerful and unified work if the reader is given enough information to understand the "system" of author, narrator and protagonist in which he finds himself.   The danger is that the writer may ignore his audience totally and identify himself too closely with narrator and protagonist resulting in a work that is self-indulgent and obscure.

In this sense, although the term symbolist may be useful in discussing such works as *A Rebours, Petersburg, The Triumph of Death*, and *A Legend in Creation*, I do not believe it can be applied to *The Petty Demon*.   Despite the expanded role of the narrator in the novel, the narrator-author is not identified with the protagonist in this intense way, but rather, addresses himself to the reader.   In fact, it is Sologub's transcendence of his preoccupation with the Peredonov within himself that enables him to show us the Peredonov within each of us with such devastating power.

One cannot call *The Petty Demon* either a decadent or a symbolist novel; nonetheless it bears the unmistakable stamp of its times.   For one thing, an anti-decadent novel could only be written while decadent values were current.   For another, the narrator in his expanded role follows the symbolist paradigm of artist-priest.   More generally, the novel shows the influence of symbolism in its rejection of realism in order to convey a higher truth.   In its originality, in its very divergences from decadent and symbolist norms, one can see in this novel the influence of a literary movement that was based in an impatience with all stylistic and metaphysical limits.

Chapter 10
Conclusion

It has been the purpose of this study to come to some understanding of the peculiar power of Sologub's novel *The Petty Demon* through an analysis of its structure. Written during a time of expansion and experimentation in the novel genre, *The Petty Demon* in form is both unique and uniquely suited to Sologub's design. Realistic values are reversed and Sologub gives us narration and setting which are complex and disturbing, and plot and characters which are flat.

Nevertheless, it is the zombielike character of Peredonov who dominates the novel (as well as this study). Peredonov's grotesque charisma and archetypal power make him more memorable than most realistic heroes. He has the insubstantial but very immediate quality of an hallucination because it is we who give him life. It takes a great deal of concentration to read *The Petty Demon*—to follow the strange plot, fathom the peculiar characters, and overcome our resistance to the unpleasant world we encounter. But this expenditure of energy on our part—this need to read actively instead of passively—lifts the novel out of the world of art and makes it an experience, and not a pastime. In some way this disturbing novel becomes part of us.

The craziness of Peredonov and the strange atmosphere of his world are created principally through Sologub's use of language. For example, Peredonov's confusion of pattern with meaning seems less bizarre to us because it is echoed, and in a sense lent credibility by the derangements of language and logic we see in other characters, an impressively large number of whom have some linguistic or verbal peculiarity. Tishkov speaks in rhymed couplets, Volodin bleats, Dar'ia shrieks, the D.A. shouts. Varvara repeats "*ty valiaesh petrushku*" ("You're playing the fool"). Rutilov creates a warped reality through false syllogisms. In Chapter 4 he silences Peredonov by telling him, "Two times two is four, therefore you must marry one of my sisters." He later "proves" to Peredonov that he is a pig because Peredonov has a five-kopeck piece (in

Russian the same word as snout).   Volodin's constant warping of language and logic is less deliberate and thus even more disorienting.   For example he proves that he is not poor in the following way: "I have never yet asked anyone for bread, and you know that 'Only the devil without a piece of bread to eat is poor' and since I not only eat a piece of bread, but even eat it with a piece of butter, I am not poor" (216).   In this context, Peredonov almost seems normal.[1]

Beyond the distortions of language and logic in the other characters, however, Peredonov is given his peculiar life by the language of the narration.   Language is the only material a novelist has with which to create a world.   The triumph of pattern over meaning, the echoing of Peredonov's derangement on a verbal level in the narration, as discussed above, creates a distorted world in which Peredonov seems real.   Perhaps the early reviewers confused Peredonov with Sologub because they sensed a peculiarity in the way the narrator mediates between author and protagonist—a partial participation of the narrator (and by extension Sologub) in Peredonov's derangement.   What they did not wish to acknowledge was their own involuntary submersion in Peredonov's deranged and lifeless view of the world.

If the novel as a whole expresses Sologub's belief that people live dead lives, the form of the novel provides an antidote.   Unlike realistic novels, The Petty Demon does not hide its workings but rather displays them.   By not allowing us to lose ourselves in the novel, by focusing our attention on the medium, on the fact that this is an artifact, Sologub forces us to reexamine our unthinking assumptions about novels and perhaps about life.   For the time that we read the novel, at least, we experience the here and now in a fresh, if disturbing, way.

The Petty Demon is a tour de force.   It is not surprising that in the several novels he wrote afterward Sologub was never able to duplicate his feat: to create and adhere to new and effective novelistic conventions expressive of a novel's meaning.   Russian literature is famous for one-of-a-kind novels: *Evgenii Onegin*, Pushkin's novel in verse, *Dead Souls*, Gogol's long poem in prose, *A Double Life*, Karolina Pavlova's sketch in poetry and prose, and *War and Peace*, Tolstoy's unique philosophical, historical epic.   To this list we must add *The Petty Demon*, Sologub's eccentric and powerful evocation of madness as a logical extension of the pettiness within us all.

In the seventy-five years since its publication *The Petty Demon* has remained a controversial novel both in Russia and the West. In the Soviet Union where printing is a government monopoly, Sologub is considered decadent and hence unworthy of publication. As early as 1926 he was denied permission to publish a book of poetry by the Soviet government.[2] Yet despite an officially imposed ban on Sologub's many novels, essays, short stories and outstanding poetry (relaxed only to publish one book of his poems in 1939 and one in 1978), *The Petty Demon* has been republished three times—in 1925, 1933, and 1958. This is in keeping with the Soviet policy of whenever possible resurrecting and, if necessary, reinterpreting great works of Russian literature.[3] Apparently the value of *The Petty Demon* as literature is considered to outweigh the political embarrassment of reprinting it.

Nonetheless, very few mentions of Sologub or studies of the novel have appeared in the Soviet Union since the Revolution. The writings about him generally consist of a few mentions in memoirs; criticism of his work appears principally in introductions to new editions and often includes awkward attempts to reconcile Sologub with the official policy of socialistic realism. A notable exception is "Fedor Sologub," an essay by Evgenii Zamiatin, a politically courageous writer of the '20s who eventually emigrated. Zamiatin draws several parallels between Sologub and Blok (who was well thought of by the new Soviet government), and describes Sologub as a truly Russian writer, although one who has learned a great deal from European literature.[4]

If frequency of translation is an indication of the popularity of an author abroad, then *The Petty Demon* has been growing in popularity in the West since 1960. According to the *Index translationum*, the novel has been translated into English (1916 and twice in 1962), French (1949 and 1967), Norwegian (1949), Danish (1964), Italian (1966), German (1969), Spanish (1969), Czech (1970), Dutch (1972), Polish (1973), Swedish (1973), Rumanian (1975) and even Japanese (1972). Many of Sologub's other works have within the last few years appeared for the first time in English, among them *Tiazhelie sny* (*Bad Dreams*) and *Tvorimaia legenda* (*A Legend in Creation*)—the novels that respectively preceded and followed *The Petty Demon*. Furthermore, since 1960 Sologub has been the subject of at least six Ph.D. dissertations, several articles and two studies, *Fedor Sologubs Roman-Trilogie* by Johannes Holthusen, and *Sologub's Literary Children* by Stanley

Rabinowitz.   And there are doubtless more to come.

Part of the reason for the growth in interest in this novel (and in the Russian symbolist movement in general) may be a result of the change in social attitudes brought about in the 1960s, which in many ways paralleled the symbolist age.   In both periods the individual became more important in relation to society, experience was valued for its own sake, and there was great interest in religion, personal transcendence through drugs, music, sex, violence and death.   Sologub's preoccupation with magic, fantasy, sexual liberation, even the sado-masochistic elements in some of his work became very stylish.   While the best of Sologub's works—of which *The Petty Demon* is one—continue to be read under any circumstances, they can have far more meaning to readers in the context of his work as a whole, and in an atmosphere in which Sologub is studied, understood, and appreciated.

Notes

Chapter 1

[1] An exception was an effusive review of the incomplete novel by L. Annibal, "Obozrenie russkikh zhurnalov (F. Sologub, *Melkii bes*)," *Vesy*, 9–10 (1905), 81–85.

[2] Nikolai Gumilev, "Khronika," *Apollon*, No. 9 (1910), 35.

[3] I have relied on the following sources for the historical information in this chapter: Patrick L. Alston, *Education and the State in Tsarist Russia* (Stanford: Stanford University Press, 1969); Robert F. Byrnes, *Pobedonostsev: His Life and Thought* (Bloomington: Indiana University Press, 1968); Richard Denis Charques, *The Twilight of Imperial Russia* (London: Oxford University Press, 1965); Charles Lowe, *Alexander III of Russia* (London: William Heinemann, 1895); Nicholas V. Riasonovsky, *History of Russia* (Oxford: Oxford University Press, 1977); Graham Stevenson, *Russia From 1812 to 1945* (New York: Praeger, 1970).

[4] "Unynie i pessimizm," *Severnyi vestnik*, No. 2 (1885), 36–50. Further citations are from 37–38 and 42–48.

[5] Byrnes, 352, 293, 295.

[6] Byrnes, 144–145; 166, 239.

[7] Alston, 80–112, 118; Nicholas Hans, *History of Russian Educational Policy, 1701–1917* (London: P. S. King & Son, 1931), 154.

[8] Fedor Sologub, *Melkii bes* (Chicago: Russian Language Specialties, 1966), 146. Future citations in parentheses after text refer to this edition. Translations unless otherwise noted are mine.

[9] Quoted in English in Byrnes, 247.

[10] Alston, 129–142.

[11] Hans, 113, 118; Stephenson, 115.

[12] See *Five Sisters: Women Against the Tsar*, ed. and trans. by Barbara Alpern Engel and Clifford N. Rosenthal (New York: Schoken, 1977).

[13] Stephenson, 115.

[14] Lowe, 191–192; Byrnes, 212, 206, 291.

[15] Bynres, 291.

[16] Byrnes, 247.

[17] P. A. Kogan, *Ocherki po istorii noveishei russkoi literatury* (Moscow: 1911), t. 3, vypusk I, 116.

[18] Byrnes, 260; Charques, 31.

[19] Iurii N. Tynianov, "Literaturnyi fakt," and "O literaturnoi evoliutsii," *Arkhaisty i novatory* (1929; rpt. Munchen: Wilhelm Fink Verlag, 1967), 5–48.

[20]John Cournos, "Fedor Sologub," *The Fortnightly Review*, Sept. 1915, 480.

[21]I use "neo-realistic" here and elsewhere in this book to designate those late nineteenth- and early twentieth-century writers whose social engagement contrasted with the neo-romantic tendencies of the symbolists. The term should not be confused with "Neo-Realism" presently applied with increasing frequency to the writings of Zamiatin, Remizov, Prisvin and others.

[22]Irwin Weil, *Gorky: His Literary Development and Influence on Soviet Intellectual Life* (New York: Random House, 1966), 9.

[23]Martin P. Rice, *Valery Briusov and the Rise of Russian Symbolism* (Ann Arbor: Ardis, 1975), 28, 31–37.

[24]Gurevich movingly describes her years of glory and suffering as owner of *Severnyi vestnik* from 1890 to its demise under severe political and financial pressure in September 1898 in "Istoriia Severnogo vestnika," *Russkaia literatura XX veka*, ed. by S. A. Vengerov (1914; rpt. Munchen: Wilhelm Fink Verlag, 1972), I, 235–264. Further information about the role of *Severnyi vestnik* in creating an audience for Russian symbolism can be found in P. V. Kupriianovskii, "Iz istorii rannego russkogo simvolizma (Simvolisty i zhurnal "Severnyi vestnik"), *Russkaia literatura XX veka (Dooktiabr'skii period)* (Kaluga, 1968), 149–173 and V. Evgen'ev–Maksimov and D. Maksimov, "Severnyi vestnik i simvolisty," *Iz proshlogo russkoi zhurnalistiki: stat'i i materialy* (Leningrad: 1930), 83–128.

[25]"Iskusstvo nashikh dnei," *Russkaia mysl'*, No. 12 (1915), 36–37, 61–62; "F. Sologub o simvolizme," *Biulleteni literatury i zhizni*, No. 14 (1914), 835; "Demony poetov," *Pereval*, May 1907, 48–51, Dec. 1907, 46–49.

[26]Several prominent and not so prominent writers have described Sologub, his relations with other symbolists and his salon in their memoires. Among them are Georgii Chulkov, "Dymnyi ladan," *Sobranie sochinenii* (St. Petersburg: Shipovnik, 1905–1911), V, 23–70, and "Fedor Sologub," *Zvezda*, No. 1 (1928), 89–100; Ilia Ehrenburg, *People and Life*, trans. by Anna Bostok and Yvonne Kapp (London: MacGibbon & Key, 1961), 87; Kornei Chukovskii, *Chukokkala* (Iskusstvo, 1979), 136–150, esp. 142–147; Konstantin Fedin, *Gorky sredi nas, Sobranie sochinenii* (Moscow: 1969), X, 256–265; Zinaida Gippius, *Zhivie litsa* (Prague: Plamia, 1925), 95–113; V. F. Khodasevich, *Nekropol': Vospominaniia* (Bruxelles: E. Gelezniakoff, 1939), 158–178. Also see Heinrich Baran, "Sologub Among the Symbolists: From the Drafts for Sologub's *Tvorimaja legenda*," *Neue Russische Literatur*, 2–3 (1979–80), 179–202.

[27]G. J. Thurston finds many more allusions to Nietzsche in his interesting but controversial article, "Sologub's *Melkij bes*," *Slavic and East European Review*, 55, No. 1 (1977), 30–44.

[28]James D. West, *Russian Symbolism: A Study of Vyacheslav Ivanov and the Russian Symbolist Aesthetic* (London: Methuen, 1970), 157.

[29]A full consideration of the interrelationship between symbolism and the figure of Sophia can be found in Samual D. Cioran, *Vladimir Soloviev and the Knighthood of the Divine Sophia* (Waterloo, Canada: Wilfred Laurier University Press, 1977).

[30]Temira Pachmuss, *Zinaida Hippius: An Intellectual Profile* (Carbondale: Southern Illinois University Press, 1971), 7, 116, 130.

[31]Oleg A. Maslenikov, *The Frenzied Poets: Andrey Biely and the Russian Symbolists* (Berkeley: University of California Press, 1952), 27, 120. Blok's turn-around and its effects on Bely are described in Cioran, 133–136, 175–177.

[32]West, *Symbolism*, 54.

[33]See J. D. West, "Neo-Romanticism and the Russian Symbolist Aesthetic," *Slavic and East European Review*, July 1973, 413–427.

[34]*What Is Art and Essays on Art by Tolstoy*, trans. by Aylmer Maude (Oxford: Oxford University Press, 1950), 156, 178, 176; Maksim Gorky, *Sobranie sochinenii v tridtsati tomakh* (Moscow, 1951), XIV, 253–315.

[35]Georgette Donchin, *The Influence of French Symbolism on Russian Poetry* ('s-Gravenhage: Mouton and Co., 1958), 11.

[36]Bernice Glatzer Rosenthal, "The Transformation of the Symbolist Echo: Mystical Anarchism and the Revolution of 1905," *Slavic Review*, 36 (1977), 608–627.

[37]An illustration of the personal and ideological differences which increasingly divided neo-realists and neo-romantics can be seen in the literary feud between Sologub and Gorky. In 1912, responding to "Smertiashkin," a Gorky story ridiculing Sologub and his wife, Sologub printed a lampoon entitled "Sergei Turgenev i Sharik (Nenapechatannye epizody iz romana 'Melkii bes')," ("Sergei Turgenev and Sharik [Unpublished Episodes from the Novel *The Petty Demon*]") which appeared in the Kadet (Constitutional Democrat) newspaper *Rech'* (Speech), Nos. 102 (April 15, p. 2), 108 (April 22, p. 3) and 116 (April 29, p. 2). In this piece Sologub made fun of two writers from the literary left or neo-realistic wing—Stephen Gavrilovich Skital'ets (1868–1941) and Maksim Gorky (according to the editors of Maksim Gorky, *Sobranie sochinenii v tridtsati tomakh* [Moscow, 1951], XXX, 536). Sologub inserted two characters modeled on these writers into highlights from *The Petty Demon*: the scene in which Peredonov accuses Volodin of being a sheep, the drinking party at Peredonov's apartment, the dream-relating scene at Grushina's party and the masquerade ball. Sergei Turgenev is described as a plagiarizing decadent writer who publishes Marxist stories as a matter of expediency but whose motto is "I am a poet." Gorky clearly served as the model for Sharik Skvortsov, a revolutionary writer with a very romantic style who wears only peasant blouses and calls himself "the newest person in Russia" (a reference to the subtitle of Chernyshevsky's revolutionary novel, *What Is To Be Done? Tales About New People*). In the lampoon, whenever either writer tries to express his philosophy one of the *Petty Demon* characters disagrees, laughs or yawns. Sologub suggests that although the two writers carefully distinguish themselves from each other and look down on provincial life, there is, in fact, very little difference between them, or for that matter between them and the petty inhabitants of Peredonov's world. In 1933, in response to a letter from the editors of Academiia publishing house, Gorky wrote that he had no objection to reprinting "Sergei Turgenev and Sharik" as a variant in the Soviet edition of *The Petty Demon* then being prepared if they would also reprint his 1912 story "Smertiashkin" which made fun of Sologub (Gorky, *Sobranie sochinenii*, XXX, 275). However, neither piece appeared nor did the explanatory essay that was to accompany them. Sologub's lampoon has never been reprinted.

[38]The best treatment of the continuity between the radical critics and socialistic realism is Rufus W. Mathewson, Jr., *The Positive Hero in Russian Literature* (Stanford: Stanford University Press, 1975).

[39]Kogan, 114, 119.

[40]Others who have discussed the dual nature of *The Petty Demon* are Linda J. Ivanits, "The Grotesque in Fedor Sologub's Novel *The Petty Demon*,"

Russian and Slavic Literature, ed. by Richard Freeborn, R. R. Milner–Gulland and Charles Ward (Cambridge: Slavica, 1976), 138; and Elizabeth Biernat [Biernatowa], " 'Maly bies' Fiodora Sologuba jako proba stworzenia modelu rosyjskiej powiesci modernistycznej," *Zeszyty naukowe wydzialu humanistycznego uniwersytetu Gdanskiego, Filologia rosyjska*, No. 3 (1973), 58.

[41]Aleksandr Blok, "O realistakh," *Sobranie sochinenii* (Moscow, 1962), V, 125; D. S. Mirsky, *A History of Russian Literature*, ed. by Francis J. Whitfield (New York: Alfred A. Knopf, 1949), 444.

Chapter 2

[1]I have based my generalizations on some thirty-five essays written before 1912 which discuss *The Petty Demon*. One excellent source for such criticism is the 1911 collection by Anastasiia Chebotarevskaia (Sologub's wife), *O Fedore Sologube: kritika, stat'i i zametki* (St. Petersburg: Shipovnik, 1911). One must be careful, however, not to accept this collection as representative of all Sologub criticism. While the essays cover a fairly broad spectrum of literary views, they all start from the premise that Sologub is a major writer who should be taken very seriously. For articles expressing a less reverent attitude toward Sologub (for example, Bely's "Dali Lama" article discussed below) one must look elsewhere.

[2]Elzbieta Biernat writes that Sologub's works in general often became pretexts for critics to argue for and against modernism. "Tworczosc Fiodora Sologuba w ocenie krytyki literackiej epoki modernizmu," *Zeszyty naukowe wydzialu humanistycznego uniwersytetu Gdanskiego, Filologia rosyjska*, No. 2 (1972), 27. Among those using reviews of the novel to advance the symbolist cause were L. Annibal, "Obozrenie russkikh zhurnalov," Aleksandr Blok, "Tvorchestvo Fedora Sologuba," *Pereval*, No. 10 (1907), 21-23 and Georgii Chulkov, "Dymnyi ladan," *Sobranie sochinenii* (St. Petersburg: Shipovnik, 1905–1911), V, 123-170. Among those attacking symbolism through criticism of the novel were Iu. M. Steklov, "O tvorchestve Fedora Sologuba," in *Literaturnyi raspad* (St. Petersburg: EOS, 1909), II, 165-216; G. S. Novopolin [Neifel'd], *Pornograficheskii element v russkoi literature* (St. Petersburg: 1909), 171-188, and A. E. Red'ko, "Fedor Sologub v bytovykh proizvedeniiakh i v 'tvorimykh legendakh,' " *Russkoe bogatstvo*, No. 2 (1909), 55-90.

[3]Vladimir Kranikhfel'd, "Literaturnye otkliki," *Sovremennyi mir*, May (1907), II, 126-135; Evgenii Anichkov, "Melkii bes," *Kriticheskoe obozrenie*, No. 3 (1907), 29-33. P. A. Kogan's review, although political in orientation, shows an unusual amount of literary sensitivity as well. "Fedor Sologub," *Ocherki po istorii noveishei russkoi literatury* (Moscow: 1911), III, 102-125.

[4]P. Orlovskii [pseudonym of V. V. Vorovskii] in a review of *Nav'i chary* compared Sologub to a thief plundering the dead body of the revolution and Kranikhfel'd who had written a very positive review of *The Petty Demon*, was hardly more flattering. P. Orlovskii, "V noch' posle bitvy (L. Andreev i F. Sologub)," *Sochineniia* (Moscow: 1931), II, 244-260; Vladimir Kranikhfel'd, "Novye lichiny Peredonova," *Sovremennyi mir*, January (1909), II, 51-56. For the rather complicated publishing history of Sologub's trilogy, originally called *Nav'i chary* (*Bewitchment of the Dead*) and later *Tvorimaia legenda* (*A Legend in Creation*) see Johannes Holthusen, *Fedor Sologubs Roman–Trilogie* ('s-Gravenhage: Mouton, 1960), 8ff.

[5]Some examples of reviews in which Sologub is analyzed through his work are: R. V. Ivanov-Razumnik, "Fedor Sologub," in *O Fedore Sologube*, 7–34; Kornei Chukovskii, "Fedor Sologub," in *Ot Chekhova do nashikh dnei* (Moscow: Vol'f, 1908), 168–181; Lev Shestov, "Poeziia i proza Fedora Sologuba," *Rech'*, No. 139 (1909), 2–3; V. Botsianovskii, "O Sologube, nedotykomke, Gogole, Groznom i proch.," in *O Fedore Sologube*, 142–183; A. Dolinin, "Otreshennyi (k psikhologii tvorchestva Fedora Sologuba)," *Zavety*, No. 7 (1913), 55–85; Evgenii Lundberg, "Lirika Fedora Sologuba," *Russkaia mysl'*, IV (1912), 57–82; A. G. Gornfel'd, "Fedor Sologub," *Russkaia literatura XX veka*, ed. by S. A. Vengerov (1914; rpt. Munchen: Wilhelm Fink Verlag, 1972), Part I, II, 14–64; I. Rozenfel'd, "Fedor Sologub," in *O Fedore Sologube*, 337–341. It may be that Sologub saw the irritation expressed by these critics as a back-handed compliment. In any event, several of these essays appeared in his wife's collection of criticism about him.

[6]Aleksandr Blok, "O realistakh," *Sobranie sochinenii* (Moscow, 1962), V, 125, 127.

[7]Blok, "Tvorchestvo Fedora Sologuba," 21–22.

[8]Zinaida Gippius, "Slezinka Peredonova (to chego ne znaet F. Sologub)," *O Fedore Sologube*, 71; subsequent citations are from 74 and 79.

[9]In the chapters on character and pattern I will demonstrate that Peredonov, far from being a source of discomfort for Sologub, was a fully intentional and masterful depiction of the dangers of self-isolation and thus is the key to Sologub's purpose in writing the novel. For the moment I will only mention that A. G. Gornfel'd refutes Gippius by citing those passages in the novel that explain and defend Peredonov in his article, "Fedor Sologub," in *Russkaia literatura XX veka*, Part I, II, 48ff.

[10]Viacheslav Ivanov, "Razskazy tainovidtsa," *Vesy*, August (1904), 48; subsequent citation, 50.

[11]Andrei Bely, "Istlevaiushchie lichiny," *O Fedore Sologube*, 96; subsequent citations 97 and 98.

[12]V. F. Khodasevich, *Nekropol': Vospominaniia* (Bruxelles: Imprimerie E. Gelezniakoff, 1939), 173–174; but Bely claimed the incident was forgotten in *Nachalo veka* (1933; rpt. Chicago: Russian Language Specialists, 1966), 446.

[13]Andrei Bely, "Dalai-lama iz Sapozhka," *Vesy*, No. 3 (1908), 74; subsequent citations from 76.

[14]The correspondence among Sologub, Valerii Briusov and Bely following the publication of "The Dali Lama of Sapozhok" further illuminates both Sologub's feelings about the article and Bely's ambivalence toward Sologub. On April 12, 1908, shortly after the article appeared, Sologub complained about it to Briusov, the nominal editor-in-chief of *Vesy*, citing as particularly offensive the sentence, "Sologub's magic is a flea bite . . . he himself . . . is not much more than a flea." Sologub was also annoyed that Bely called him "Fedor Kuz'mich" in the article—Sologub never used his patronymic as part of his penname—thus compromising his anonymity. Briusov replied three days later and tried to soothe Sologub by pointing to the positive statements about him in the article. Sologub stiffly rejoined on April 19 that "the comparison of me to a flea perhaps is very true, but it is intolerable in the pages of a journal to which I contribute"—an implied threat to quit *Vesy*. On April 30 Bely, at Briusov's prompting, wrote Sologub an apology which was even more ambivalent than the article.

Bely, like Briusov, quoted the phrases in the article complimentary to Sologub and added, "I am deeply amazed, Fedor Kuz'mich, that you consider yourself offended by my article." Apparently feeling that the best defense is a good offense, Bely next professed himself to be very offended because Sologub had not approached him directly with his complaints. Sologub, he wrote, had revealed his snobbishness and lack of respect for Bely. Bely then defended his article on the grounds that he was a writer as well a critic and therefore had to challenge and defeat Sologub's art for the sake of his own: "If I were only a critic, if I didn't have my own *holy things* for which I am prepared to surrender my life, I would only have stated your significance in literature; but as a soldier I am obliged to draw my sword for my *own* things . . . ." (italics Bely's). In conclusion, Bely offered to print an apology for any phrases Sologub found objectionable, and, if necessary, quit *Vesy* rather than allow Sologub to do so. He ended somewhat hysterically, "I await your answer. Understand that my pure-hearted communication to you demands that you calm me with an answer, no matter what the character of that response. I can be destroyed as a poet or as a literary critic—that's not the point; in this I look upon you as a dear teacher. There is only one area in which I address you as an equal—this is the area of honor and moral relations." Was Bely suggesting his readiness to fight a duel? Strange as this suggestion seems, less than two years before, in August 1906, Bely had challenged Aleksandr Blok to a duel that was prevented by Blok's wife, Liubov' Dmietrievna, who was the occasion of the quarrel. Here, however, Bely probably just indulged in some self-dramatization. In any case, on May 1 Sologub sent Bely a stiff but somewhat mollified reply in which he repeated his objections to the article, calling Bely's comparisons of him "not true or appropriate" and Bely's reductionistic tables "witty but totally arbitrary" and there the matter was allowed to drop (S. S. Grechishkin and A. B. Lavrov, "Andrei Bely: pis'ma k F. Sologubu," *Ezhegodnik rukopisnogo otdela pushkinskogo doma na 1972* [Leningrad, 1974], 131–137).

[15]Discussions of Sologub's solipsism occur in A. Dolinin, "Otreshennyi," 79; Modest Gofman, *Kniga o russkikh poetakh poslednego desiatiletiia: ocherki, stikhotvoreniia, avtografii* (1909), 247; A. G. Gornfel'd, "Fedor Sologub," *Russkaia literatura XX veka*, 16, 63; R. V. Ivanov-Razumnik, "Fedor Sologub," *O Fedore Sologube*, 27–28, among others.

[16]I am thinking specifically of the above-mentioned poems, "Gimny stradaiushchego Dionisa," *Novyi put'*, January 1904, 135–142 as well as " 'Ia,' Kniga sovreshennogo samoutverzhdeniia," *Zolotoe runo*, No. 2 (1906), 76–79; "Liturgiia mne," a dramatic piece with similar themes which appeared in *Vesy*, No. 2 (1907), 9–21; the essay "Chelovek cheloveku–d'iavol," *Zolotoe runo*, No. 1 (1907), 53–55 and connected aesthetic essays: "Elisaveta," *Vesy*, No. 11 (1905), 25–29; "Teatr odnoi voli," *Kniga o novom teatre: Sbornik statei* (St. Petersburg: Shipovnik, 1908), 179–198.

[17]Georgii Chulkov, "Dymnyi ladan," 26.

[18]Ilya Ehrenburg, *People and Life*, trans. by Anna Bostok and Yvonne Kapp (London: MacGibbon & Key, 1961), 87; Chulkov, "Fedor Sologub," *Zvezda*, No. 1 (1928), 89; Konstantin Fedin, *Gorky sredi nas* in *Sobranie sochinenii* (Moscow, 1968), X, 256–257; Andrew Field, *The Complection of Russian Literature* (New York: Antheneum, 1971), 297; A. E. Red'ko, "Fedor Sologub v bytovykh proizvedeniiakh i v 'tvorimykh legendakh,' " 55–56.

[19]Dolinin, Gornfel'd, Chukovskii, Steklov and Novopolin all identify Peredonov with Sologub. Discussions of Sologub's decadence and morbidity

can be found in Gornfel'd, Steklov, Chulkov, Chukovskii, Lundberg, Dolinin, Shestov and Rozenfel'd. Suggestions that Sologub needs a psychiatrist or is insane appear in G. S. Novopolin, 187–188; Iu. M. Steklov, 176; A. G. Gornfel'd, 63; A. Izmailov, "Zagadka sfinksa," *Literturnyi olimp* (Moscow, 1911), 316 and E. Karamzina-Artsikhovskaia, "O Fedore Sologube kak ob odnom iz predstavitelei psikhopatologicheskogo techeniia sovremennoi russkoi khudozhestvennoi literatury," *Vestnik psikhologii, kriminal'noi antropologii i gipnotizma*, vyp. 5 (1908), 223–244.

[20]Evgenii Lundberg, "Lirika Fedora Sologuba," *Russkaia mysl'*, IV (1912), 60; Dolinin, "Otreshennyi," 84.

[21]See Modest Gofman, *Kniga o russkikh poetakh*, 241ff. The first biography of Sologub, written by his wife, Anastasiia Chebotarevskaia, appeared in S. A. Vengerov, *Russkaia literatura XX veka*, Part I, Vol. II, 9–13.

[22]Iu. I. Aikhenval'd, "Bibliograficheskii otdel," *Russkaia mysl'*, No. 9 (1907), III, 171 admits to feeling "suffocated and nauseous" while reading the novel; Shestov, 2, found the novel "revolting."

[23]Several critics wrote about Sologub repeatedly, among them A. G. Gornfel'd, "Nedotykomka," *Knigi i liudi* (St. Petersburg: Zhizhn', 1908), I, 32–40, "Plamennyi krug," *Zarnitsy* (St. Petersburg, 1909), II, 53–88, "F. Sologub," *Russkaia literatura XX veka*, II, 14–64, and "Temnyi put'" (k shestidesiatiletiiu F. Sologuba)," *Rossiia*, No. 6 (1923), 27–29; G. Chulkov, "Faust i Melkii bes," *Rech'*, No. 301 (1908), 3, "Dymnyi ladan," *Pokryvalo Izidy* (Moscow: Zolotoe runo, 1909), 58–63, "Glukhie vystrely," *Nashi sputniki* (Moscow: N. V. Vasil'ev, 1922), 44–53; A. E. Red'ko, "F. Sologub v bytovykh proizvedeniiakh i 'tvorimykh legendakh,' " *Russkoe bogatstvo*, No. 2 (1909), II, 65–101, "Eshche problema," *Russkoe bogatstvo*, No. 1 (1910), II, 130–144, "C 'Perevala' v 'Shipovnik' (F. Sologub, *Sobranie sochinenii*, t. VIII)," *Russkoe bogatstvo*, No. 10 (1910), II, 154–157.

Chapter 3

[1]Douglas Hewitt, *The Approach to Fiction: Good and Bad Readings of Novels* (London: Longman, 1972), 1. Problems with the poetics of the novel are discussed by Percy Lubbock, *The Craft of Fiction* (London: Jonathan Cape, 1921), 5–22; Philip Stevick, *Theory of the Novel* (New York: The Free Press, 1967), 1; Joseph Warren Beach, *The Twentieth-Century Novel: Studies in Technique* (New York: Appleton-Century-Crofts, 1932), 3–4; Robert Alter, *Fielding and the Nature of the Novel* (Cambridge: Harvard University Press, 1968), 106, 180.

[2]Edwin Muir, *The Structure of the Novel* (New York: Harcourt Brace and World Inc., 1969), 41, 24; Hewitt, 105; Alvin J. Seltzer, *Chaos in the Novel, the Novel in Chaos* (New York: Schocken Books, 1974), 10.

[3]René Wellek and Austin Warren in *Theory of Literature* (New York: Harcourt Brace and World Inc., 1956), 216 consider character, plot and setting as the constituents of the novel. I have added narration as a fourth constituent because it is central to a definition of the novel as an extended prose narrative.

[4]J. P. Stern, *On Realism* (London: Routledge & Kegan Paul, 1973), 31.

[5]Maurice Z. Shroder, "The Novel as a Genre," *Theory of the Novel*, ed.

by Philip Stevick (New York: The Free Press, 1967), 14. Shroder here is discussing novels in general, but his statement applies most immediately to realistic novels.

[6]Stern, 142.

[7]Seltzer, 11.

[8]Discussions of the twentieth-century sense of the relativity of truth and its effect on novels can be found in Stevick, 27 and in Robert Scholes and Robert Kellogg, *The Nature of Narrative* (Oxford: Oxford University Press, 1966), 274, 276. Hewitt describes the effects of the sense of individual isolation and the loss of a sense of common reality in *The Approach to Fiction*, 78.

[9]Stern, 142.

[10]See Seltzer's discussion of the elusiveness of truth and character in *Lord Jim*, 80–91.

[11]Fyodor Sologub, *Bad Dreams*, trans. by Vassar W. Smith (Ann Arbor: Ardis, 1978), 3, 4, 18, 22.

Chapter 4

[1]E. M. Forster, *Aspects of the Novel* (New York: Harcourt Brace & Co., 1927), 97; also 75–96.

[2]Forster, 103–108.

[3]Elizabeth Drew, *The Novel: A Modern Guide to 15 English Masterpieces* (New York: W. W. Norton, 1963), 19.

[4]Stern, *On Realism*, 72–73; Hewitt, *The Approach to Fiction*, 45–58; Scholes and Kellogg, *The Nature of Narrative*, 161.

[5]Muir, *The Structure of the Novel*, 141–146; citation is from 142.

Chapter 5

[1]The deleted variant appears in *Melkii bes* (Chicago: Russian Language Specialities, 1966), 429–432.

[2]These generalizations are based on the 1914 Sirin edition of *Melkii bes*, published as part of Sologub's *Collected Works* and overseen by Sologub himself.

[3]A. G. Gornfel'd, "Fedor Sologub," 48.

[4]Forster, *Aspects of the Novel*, 155–156; 142.

[5]Forster, 228–234.

Chapter 6

[1]R. D. Laing, *The Politics of Experience* (New York: Ballantine Books, 1967), 113–118. Also see Laing's *The Divided Self* (Baltimore: Penguin Books, 1968), 80 and 90.

[2]*Tree and Leaf* (Boston: Houghton Mifflin Company, 1965), 46–55.

[3]Linda Ivanits also discusses this parallel in "The Grotesque in Fedor Sologub's Novel, *The Petty Demon*," *Russian and Slavic Literature*, ed. by Richard Freeborn, R. R. Milner-Gulland, Charles Award (Cambridge: Slavica, 1976), 149–150.

[4]Discussions of Gogol's influence on Sologub may be found in Andrei Bely, "Gogol' i Sologub," *Masterstvo Gogolia* (Moscow, 1934), 291–294; Andrew Field, Translator's Preface to *The Petty Demon* (Bloomington: University of Indiana Press, 1970), xx–xxi, John Cournos, "Fedor Sologub," 489.

[5]Discussions of the influence of Dostoevsky on Sologub in relation to the problem of evil can be found in Helen Muchnic, "Visions, Dreams and Nightmares: Russian Literature in the 1890s," *Russian Writers: Notes and Essays* (New York: Random House, 1963), 212–221; Zinaida Gippius, 70–78; R. Ivanov-Razumnik, "Fedor Sologub," *O Sologube*, 25, and Stanley Rabinowitz, *Sologub's Literary Children: Key to a Symbolist's Prose* (Columbus: Slavica, 1980).

Chapter 7

[1]Discussed in Erich Auerbach, *Mimesis*, trans. by Willard R. Trask (Princeton University Press, 1953), 468–492.

Chapter 8

[1]Wayne Booth goes so far as to insert an additional persona between the narrator and author, namely an "implied author," whom he defines as a "created second self, bigger than the narrator and smaller than the author as man." The implied author, he writes, represents the "core of norms and choices in the novel" and changes with each work. *The Rhetoric of Fiction* (Chicago: University of Chicago Press, 1961), 73–74.

[2]For example, Dolinin, 70; Gornfel'd, 46; Steklov, 176; Novopolin, 178; Chukovsky, "Fedor Sologub," 179.

[3]An excellent discussion of realistic narrators and their transformation by Henry James and James Joyce can be found in Robert Scholes and Robert Kellogg, *The Nature of Narrative* (Oxford: Oxford University Press, 1966), 268–274. Two works that more generally examine the evolution of narrative from realism to modernism are Alvin Seltzer, *Chaos in the Novel, the Novel in Chaos*, and Erich Kahler, *The Inward Turn of Narrative*, trans. by Richard and Clara Winston (Princeton: Princeton University Press, 1973).

[4]In translating this opening paragraph into English I have had to take liberties with verb tenses in order to be faithful to the tone. In the Russian all the verbs appear in the imperfective aspect, something which sounds perfectly normal to the Russian ear, as this is a description, but which, if translated literally into English, would sound most peculiar.

[5]Douglas Hewitt, *The Approach to Fiction: Good and Bad Readings of Novels* (London: Longman, 1972), 54, 55.

NOTES

Chapter 9

[1]D. S. von Mohrenschildt, "The Russian Symbolist Movement," *PMLA*, 53 (1938), 1197 and Georgette Donchin, *The Influence of French Symbolism on Russian Poetry* ('s–Gravenhage: Mouton and Co., 1958), 94.

[2]For example D. M. Merezhkovsky, "Griadushchii Kham," *Polnoe sobranie sochinenii* (St. Petersburg: 1911), XI, 1–36; Andrei Bely, "Apokalipsis v russkoi poezii," *Vesy*, No. 4 (1905), 13–14.

[3]Kenneth Cornell, "The Symbolist Movement," *Yale Romanic Series*, series 2, no. 2 (New Haven: Yale University Press, 1951) 45; Georgette Donchin, *The Influence of French Symbolism on Russian Poetry*, 11. James West has a good sampling of how various Russian symbolists differentiated symbolists from decadents in *Russian Symbolism* (London: Methuen & Co., 1970), 191, n 1.

[4]Donchin, 120–150.

[5]Albert–Marie Schmidt, *La littérature symboliste (1870–1900)* (Paris: Presses Universitaires de France, 1969), 37.

[6]J.-K. Huysmans, *A Rebours* (Paris: Fasquelle, 1970), 269.

[7]*Tvorimaia legenda* (1914; rpt. Munchen: Wilhelm Fink Verlag, 1972), III, 186.

[8]Anna Balakian, *The Symbolist Movement* (New York: Random House, 1967), 158.

[9]Johannes Holthusen, *Fedor Sologubs Roman-Trilogie* ('s–Gravenhage: Mouton, 1960), 18; Galina Selegen', *Prekhitraia viaz: Simvolizm v russkoi proze: Melkii bes* (Washington, D.C., Kamkin, 1968), 124.

[10]Robert A. Maguire and John E. Malmstad in discussing Bely's *Petersburg* find this closed system of author, narrator, and characters typical of symbolist novels: "There are no private thoughts or actions in *Petersburg*; all are reflexes of larger realities, which in turn are experienced by all the characters . . . . The world of the novel is ultimately a closed world in which every point bears on every other." Introduction, *Petersburg* by Andrei Bely, translated, annotated and introduced by Robert A. Maguire and John E. Malmstad (Bloomington: Indiana University Press, 1978), xii, xviii.

Chapter 10

[1]For more detailed discussion of Sologub's use of language in *The Petty Demon* see Selegen', 158–204.

[2]See A. Volkov, *Poeziia russkogo imperializma* (Moscow, 1935), 52–53, and *Bol'shaia sovetskaia entsiklopediia*, 1957, XL, 45 for attacks on Sologub's decadence.

For an account of Sologub's problems with the censorship after the early 1920s and of how his papers were safeguarded after his death see R. Ivanov-Razumnik, *Pisatel'skie sud'by* (New York: literaturnyi fond, 1951), 14–17.

[3]See Maurice Friedberg, *Russian Classics in Soviet Jackets* (New York: Columbia University Press, 1962) for a study of the attitude of the Soviet government toward pre-Revolutionary classics.

[4]Evgenii Zamiatin, "Fedor Sologub," *Litsa* (1924; rpt. in New York: Mezhdunarodnoe Literaturnoe Sodruzhestvo, 1967), 29-37.

A particularly fine example of the problems of applying socialist realist criticism to Sologub can be found in M. I. Dikman's Introductory Essay to *Stikhotvoreniia (Poems)* of Fedor Sologub (Leningrad: Biblioteka Poeta, 1978), 17. In her otherwise excellent essay Dikman writes that Sologub's decadence is "a consequence of a steadfast disassociation of his personality from an oppressive social situation . . . . Behind it is the typical agony of life in [pre-Revolutionary Russian] society." Thus, Sologub, who lived in great luxury as soon as he could afford to do so, who strenuously opposed the 1917 Bolshevik Revolution and tried to emigrate afterwards, is transformed into a struggling victim of capitalist exploitation and even an unconscious revolutionary.

List of Works Cited

Aikhenval'd, Iu. I. "Fedor Sologub." *Russkaia mysl'*, No. 9 (1907), III, 170–172.

Alston, Patrick L. *Education and the State in Tsarist Russia.* Stanford: Stanford University Press, 1969.

Alter, Robert. *Fielding and the Nature of the Novel.* Cambridge: Harvard University Press, 1968.

_____. *Partial Magic: The Novel as a Self-Conscious Genre.* Berkeley: University of California Press, 1975.

Anichkov, Evgenii. "Melkii bes," *Kriticheskoe obozrenie*, No. 3 (1907), 29–33. Also in Chebotarevskaia, *O Sologube*, 217–221.

Annibal, L. "Obozrenie russkikh zhurnalov (F. Sologub, *Melkii bes*)," *Vesy*, Nos. 9–10 (1905), 81–85.

Auerbach, Eric. *Mimesis*, trans. by Willard R. Trask. Princeton: Princeton University Press, 1953.

Balakian, Anna. *The Symbolist Movement.* New York: Random House, 1967.

Baran, Henryk. "Trirodov Among the Symbolists: From the Drafts for Sologub's *Tvorimaja legenda.*" *Neue Russische Literatur*, 2–3 (1979–80), 179–202.

Beach, Joseph Warren. *The Twentieth-Century Novel: Studies in Technique.* New York: Appleton-Century-Crofts, 1932.

Bely, Andrei [Bugaev]. "Apokalipsis v russkoi poezii," *Vesy*, No. 4 (1905), 11–28.

_____. "Dalai-lama iz Sapozhka," *Vesy*, No. 3 (1908), 64–76.

_____. "Istlevaiushchie lichiny," in *O Fedore Sologube: kritika, stat'i i zametki.* St. Petersburg: Shipovnik, 1911, 96–98.

_____. *Masterstvo Gogolia.* Moscow: 1934; 291–294.

_____. *Nachalo veka.* 1933; reprint. Chicago: Russian Language Specialities, 1966.

Biernat, Elzbieta [Biernatowa]. "Tworczosc Fiodora Sologuba w ocenie krytyki literackiej epoki modernizmu," *Zeszyty naukowe wydzialu humanistycznego uniwersytetu Gdanskiego, Filologia rosyjska*, No. 2 (1972), 19–38.

_____. "'Maly bies' Fiodora Sologuba jako proba stworzenia modelu rosyjskiej powiesci modernistycznej," *Zeszyty naukowe wydzialu humanistycznego uniwersytetu Gdanskiego, Filologia rosyjska*, No. 3 (1973), 55–69.

Blok, Aleksandr. "O realistakh," *Sobranie sochinenii.* Moscow: 1962, V, 99–129.

_____. "Tvorchestvo Fedora Sologuba," *Pereval*, No. 10 (1907), 21–23.

Booth, Wayne. *The Rhetoric of Fiction.* Chicago: University of Chicago Press, 1961.

Botsianovskii, V. "O Sologube, nedotykomke, Gogole, Groznom i proch." *O Fedore Sologube: kritika, stat'i i zametki.* St. Petersburg: Shipovnik, 1911,

142–183.

Byrnes, Robert F. *Pobedonostsev: His Life and Thought.* Bloomington: Indiana University Press, 1968.

Charques, Denis. *The Twilight of Imperial Russia.* London: Oxford University Press, 1965.

Chebotarevskaia, Anastasiia, ed. *O Fedore Sologube: kritika, stat'i i zametki.* St. Petersburg: Shipovnik, 1911.

———. "Biograficheskaia spravka." In *Russkaia literatura XX veka.* Ed. by S. A. Vengerov. 1914; rpt. Munchen: Wilhelm Fink Verlag, 1972, Part I, II, 9–13.

Chukovskii, Kornei. "Fedor Sologub," *Ot Chekhova do nashikh dnei.* St. Petersburg: Vol'f, 1908, 168–181.

———. "Putevoditel' po Sologubu," *Sobranie sochinenii,* Moscow: 1969, VI, 332–367.

———. *Chukokkala.* Iskusstvo, 1979.

Chulkov, Georgii. "Dymnyi ladan." *Sochineniia.* St. Petersburg: Shipovnik, 1905–1911, V. 23–30.

———. "Faust i Melkii bes." *Rech',* No. 301 (1908), 3.

———. "Fedor Sologub," *Zvezda,* No. 1 (1928), 89–100.

———. "Glukhie vystrely." *Nashi sputniki.* Moscow: N. V. Vasil'ev, 1922, 44–53.

Cioran, Samuel D. *Vladimir Soloviev and the Knighthood of the Divine Sophia.* Waterloo, Canada: Wilfred Laurier University Press, 1977.

Cornell, Kenneth. "The Symbolist Movement," *Yale Romanic Series,* series 2. New Haven: Yale University Press, 1951, no. 2.

Cournos, John. "Fedor Sologub," *The Fortnightly Review,* Sept. (1915), 480–490.

Dolinin, A. "Otreshennyi (k psikhologii tvorchestva Fedora Sologuba), *Zavety,* No. 7 (1913), 55–85.

Donchin, Georgette. *The Influence of French Symbolism on Russian Poetry.* 's–Gravenhage: Mouton and Co., 1958.

Drew, Elizabeth. *The Novel: A Modern Guide to 15 English Masterpieces.* New York: W. W. Norton, 1963.

Ehrenburg, Ilya. *People and Life,* trans. by Anna Bostok and Yvonne Kapp. London: MacGibbon & Key, 1961.

Engel, Barbara Alpern and Rosenthal, Clifford N. *Five Sisters: Women Against the Tsar.* New York: Schoken, 1977.

Fedin, Konstantin. *Gorky sredi nas. Sobranie sochinenii.* Moscow: 1969, X.

Field, Andrew. *The Complection of Russian Literature.* New York: Antheneum, 1971.

———. Translator's Preface to *The Petty Demon.* Bloomington: University of Indiana Press, 1970.

Forster, E. M. *Aspects of the Novel.* New York: Harcourt, Brace & Co., 1927.

Friedberg, Maurice. *Russian Classics in Soviet Jackets.* New York: Columbia University Press, 1962.

Gippius, Zinaida. "Sleznika Peredonova (to chego ne znaet F. Sologub)." *O Fedore Sologube,* ed. by Anastasiia Chebotarevskaia. St. Petersburg: Shipovnik, 1911, 72–78.

_____. *Zhivie litsa.* Prague: Plamya, 1925.

Gofman, Modest. *Kniga o russkikh poetakh poslednego desiatiletiia: ocherki, stikhotvoreniia, avtografii.* St. Petersburg: 1909.

Gorky, Maksim. *Sobranie sochinenii.* Moscow: 1953–55, XXX.

Gornfel'd, A. G. "F. Sologub," *Russkaia literatura XX veka.* Ed. by S. A. Vengerov. 1914; rpt. Munchen: Wilhelm Fink Verlag, 1972. Part I, II, 14–64.

_____. "Nedotykomka." *Knigi i liudi.* St. Petersburg: Zhizn', 1908, I, 32–40.

_____. "Plamennyi krug." *Zarnitsy.* St. Petersburg, 1909, II, 53–88.

_____. "Temnyi put'. (K shestidesiatiletiiu F. Sologuba)." *Rossiia*, No. 6 (1923), 27–29.

Grechishkin, S. S. and Lavrov, A. B. "Andrei Bely: Pis'ma k F. Sologubu." *Ezhegodnik rukopisnogo otdela pushkinskogo doma na 1972.* Leningrad: 1974, 131–137.

Gumilev, Nikolai. "Khronika," *Apollon*, No. 9 (1910), 35–36.

Gurevich, Liubov'. "Istoriia Severnogo vestnika," *Russkaia literatura XX veka.* Ed. by S. A. Vengerov, 1914; rpt. Munchen: Wilhelm Fink Verlag, 1972, 235–264.

Hans, Nicholas. *History of Russian Educational Policy, 1701–1917.* London: P. S. King & Son, 1931.

Hewitt, Douglas. *The Approach to Fiction: Good and Bad Readings of Novels.* London: Longman, 1972.

Holthusen, Johannes. *Fedor Sologubs Roman-Trilogie.* 's-Gravenhage: Mouton, 1960.

Huysmans, J.-K. *A Rebours.* Paris: Fasquelle, 1970.

Ivanits, Linda J. "The Grotesque in Fedor Sologub's Novel, *The Petty Demon.*" In *Russian and Slavic Literature.* Ed. by Richard Freeborn, R. R. Milner-Gulland, and Charles A. Ward. Cambridge: Slavica, 1976, 137–174.

Ivanov (Professor). "Unynie i pessimizm," *Severnyi vestnik*, No. 2 (1885), 36–50.

Ivanov, Viacheslav. "Razskazy tainovidtsa," *Vesy*, August 1904, 47–50.

Ivanov-Razumnik, R. "Fedor Sologub." *O Fedore Sologube: kritika, stat'i i zametki.* St. Petersburg: Shipovnik, 1911, 7–34.

_____. *Pisatel'skie sud'by.* New York: literaturnyi fond, 1951.

Izmailov, A. "Zagadka sfinksa." *Literaturnyi olimp.* Moscow: 1911, 294–336.

Kahler, Erich. *The Inward Turn of Narrative.* Trans. by Richard and Clara Winston. Princeton: Princeton University Press, 1973.

Karamzina–Artsikhovskaia, E. "O F. Sologube kak ob odnom iz predstavitelei psikhopatologicheskogo techeniia sovremennoi russkoi khudozhestvennoi literatury." *Vestnik psikhologii, kriminal'noi antropologii i gipnotizma*, No. 5 (1908), 223–244.

Khodasevich, V. F. *Nekropol': Vospominaniia.* Bruxelles: Imprimerie E. Gelezniakoff, 1939.

Kogan, P. A. "Fedor Sologub." *Ocherki po istorii noveishei russkoi literatury.* Moscow: 1911, III, 102–125.

Kranikhfel'd, Vladimir. "Literaturnye otkliki." *Sovremennyi mir*, May (1907), II, 126–135.

_____. "Novye lichiny Peredonova." *Sovremennyi mir*, January (1909), II, 51-56.

Kupriianovskii, P. V. "Iz istorii rannego russkogo simvolizma (Simvolisty i zhurnal "Severnyi vestnik")." *Russkaia literatura XX veka (Dooktiabr'skii period)*. Kaluga, 1968, 149-173.

Laing, R. D. *The Divided Self*. Baltimore: Penguin Books, 1968.

_____. *The Politics of Experience*. New York: Ballantine Books, 1967.

Lowe, Charles. *Alexander III of Russia*. London: William Heineman, 1895.

Lubbock, Percy. *The Craft of Fiction*. London: Jonathan Cape, 1921.

Lundberg, Evgenii. "Lirika Fedora Sologuba." *Russkaia mysl'*, IV (1912), 57-82.

Maguire, Robert A. and Malmstad, John E., trans. *Petersburg*, by Andrei Bely. Bloomington: Indiana University Press, 1978.

Maksimov, D. and Evgen'ev-Maksimov V. "Severnyi vestnik i simvolisty." *Iz proshlogo russkoi zhurnalistiki: stat'i i materialy*, Leningrad: 1930, 83-128.

Maslenikov, Oleg A. *The Frenzied Poets: Andrey Biely and the Russian Symbolists*. Berkeley, University of California Press, 1952.

Mathewson, Rufus W., Jr. *The Positive Hero in Russian Literature*. Stanford: Stanford University Press, 1975.

Merezhkovsky, D. M. "Griadushchii Kham." *Polnoe sobranie sochinenii*. St. Petersburg: 1911, XI, 1-36.

Mohrenschildt, D. S. von. "The Russian Symbolist Movement." *PMLA*, 53 (1938), 1193-1209.

Muchnic, Helen. "Visions, Dreams and Nightmares: Russian Literature in the 1890s." *Russian Writers: Notes and Essays*. New York: Random House, 1963, 212-221.

Muir, Edwin. *The Structure of the Novel*. New York: Harcourt, Brace and World Inc., 1969.

Novopolin, G. S. [Neifel'd, G. S.]. *Pornograficheskii element v russkoi literature*. St. Petersburg: 1909, 171-188.

Orlovskii, P. [Vorovskii, V. V.]. "V noch' posle bitvy (L. Andreev i F. Sologub)." In *Sochineniia*. Moscow: 1931, II, 244-260.

Pachmuss, Temira. *Zinaida Hippius: An Intellectual Profile*. Carbondale: Southern Illinois University Press, 1971.

Rabinowitz, Stanley. *Sologub's Literary Children: Key to a Symbolist's Prose*. Columbus: Slavica, 1980.

Red'ko, A. E. "Fedor Sologub v bytovykh proizvedeniiakh i v 'tvorimykh legendakh.' " *Russkoe bogatstvo*, No. 2 (1909), II, 55-90.

_____. "Eshche problema." *Russkoe bogatstvo*, No. I (1910), II, 130-144.

_____. "C 'Perevala' v 'Shipovnik.' (F. Sologub. Sobranie sochinenii.") *Russkoe bogatstvo*, No. 10 (1910), II, 154-157.

Riasonovsky, Nicholas V. *History of Russia*. Oxford: Oxford University Press, 1977.

Rice, Martin P. *Valery Briusov and the Rise of Russian Symbolism*. Ann Arbor: Ardis, 1975.

Rosenthal, Bernice Glatzer. "Nietzsche in Russia: The Case of Merezhkovsky." *Slavic Review*, 35 (1974), 429-52.

_____. "The Transformation of the Symbolist Echo: Mystical Anarchism and the Revolution of 1905." *Slavic Review*, 36 (1977), 608-27.

Rozenfel'd, I. "F. Sologub." *O Fedore Sologube: kritika, stat'i i zametki.* St. Petersburg: Shipovnik, 1911, 337–341.

Schmidt, Albert-Marie. *La littérature symboliste (1870–1900).* Paris: Presses Universitaires de France, 1969.

Scholes, Robert and Kellog, Robert. *The Nature of Narrative.* Oxford: Oxford University Press, 1966.

Selegen', Galina. *Prekhitraia viaz: Simvolizm v russkoi proze: Melkii bes.* Washington, D.C.: Kamkin, 1968.

Seltzer, Alvin J. *Chaos in the Novel, the Novel in Chaos.* New York: Schocken Books, 1974.

Shestov, Lev [Shvartsman]. "Poeziia i proza Fedora Sologuba." *Rech'*, No. 139 (1909), 2–3. Also in Chebotarevskaia, 58–71.

Shroder, Maurice Z. "The Novel as a Genre." *Theory of the Novel.* Ed. by Philip Stevick. New York: The Free Press, 1967.

Sologub, Fedor [Teternikov]. *Bad Dreams.* Trans. by Vassar W. Smith. Ann Arbor: Ardis, 1978.

_____. "Chelovek cheloveku—d'iavol." *Zolotoe runo*, No. 1 (1907), 53–55.

_____. "Demony poetov." *Pereval*, May (1907), 48–51; Dec., 46–49.

_____. "Elisaveta." *Vesy*, No. 11 (1905), 25–29.

_____. "F. Sologub o simvolizme." *Biulleteni literatury i zhizni*, No. 14 (1914).

_____. "Gimmy stradaiushchego Dionisa." *Novyi put'*, No. 1 (1904), 135–142.

_____. " 'Ia,' Kniga sovreshennogo samoutverzhdeniia." *Zolotoe runo.* No. 2 (1906), 76–79.

_____. "Iskusstvo nashikh dnei." *Russkaia mysl'*, No. 12 (1915), 36–37, 61–62.

_____. "Liturgiia mne." *Vesy*, No. 3 (1907), 9–21.

_____. *Melkii bes.* Chicago: Russian Language Specialities, 1966.

_____. "Sergei Turgenev i Sharik." *Rech'*, No. 102 (1912), 2; No. 109 (1912), 3; No. 116 (1912), 2.

_____. *Stikhotvoreniia.* Leningrad: Biblioteka Poeta, 1978.

_____. "Teatr odnoi voli." *Kniga o novom teatre: Sbornik statei.* St. Petersburg: Shipovnik, 1908, 179–198.

_____. *Tvorimaia legenda.* 1914; rpt. Munchen: Wilhelm Fink Verlag, 1972.

Steklov, Iu. M. "O tvorchestve Fedora Sologuba." *Literaturnyi raspad.* St. Petersburg, EOS, 1909, II, 165–216.

Stern, J. P. *On Realism.* London: Routledge & Kegan Paul, 1973.

Stevenson, Graham. *Russia From 1812 to 1945.* New York: Praeger, 1970.

Stevick, Philip. *Theory of the Novel.* New York: The Free Press, 1967.

Thurston, G. F. "Sologub's *Melkij bes.*" *Slavic and East European Review*, 55, No. 1 (1977), 30–44.

Tolkien, J. R. *Tree and Leaf.* Boston: Houghton Mifflin Company, 1965.

Tolstoy, Leo. *What Is Art and Essays on Art by Tolstoy.* Trans. by Aylmer Maude. Oxford: Oxford University Press, 1950.

Tynianov, Iurii N. "Literaturnyi fakt," and "O literaturnoi evoliutsii." *Arkhaisty i novatory*, 1929; rpt. Munchen: Wilhelm Fink Verlag, 1967, 5–48.

Volkov, A. *Poeziia russkogo imperializma.* Moscow, 1935.

Weil, Irwin. *Gorky: His Literary Development and Influence on Soviet Intellectual Life.* New York: Random House, 1966.

Wellek, René and Warren, Austin. *Theory of Literature.* New York: Harcourt Brace and World Inc., 1956.

West, James D. "Neo–Romanticism and the Russian Symbolist Aesthetic." *Slavic and East European Review*, July 1973, 413–427.

_____. *Russian Symbolism: A Study of Viacheslav Ivanov and the Russian Symbolist Aesthetic.* London: Methuen, 1970.

Zamiatin, Evgenii. "Fedor Sologub." *Litsa,* 1924; rpt. New York: Mezhdunarodnoe Literaturnoe Sodruzhestvo, 1967, 29–37.

Index

Nedotykomka, 60, 70, 76, 78–79, 84

Neo-realism, 26–27, 31–34, 36, 47

Neo-romanticism, 26, 27–32; *see also* Russian symbolist movement

Nicholas II, 14

Nietzsche, Friedrich, 28, 30, 39, 44

1905 Revolution, 32, 35, 109, 111

Northern Herald, see *Severnyi vestnik*

Novel: constituents of, 48, 52; genre, 12, 25, 46, 47–53, 114; opening sentences, 103–104; patterned, 68–71; realistic, 47–50, 52, 68, 70, 91, 95, 103, 113, 114, 115; Russian, 24–25, 47, 90; symbolist, 33, 47, 108, 112–113, 128 n 10

Novyi put', 39

Ober-Procurator, 14

Oblomov (Goncharov), 26, 90, 103

Parish schools, 14, 18–20

Pattern in *TPD*, 69–71, 72–89, 95, 105–106, 115

Peredonovism, 71, 72–89; and art, 84–89; and children, 79–81, 89; and nature, 76–77, 89; and religion, 78–79, 89; and women, 82–84, 89

Père Goriot, Le (Balzac), 90, 103

Pereval (The Passage), 36

Petersburg (Bely), 33, 47, 104, 128 n 10

Petty Demon, The (Melkii bes): author's introductions, 45–46, 98; opening sentences, 104–105; publication history, 11, 35; and the realistic novel, 51, 52, 114, 115; political criticism of, 35; reception, 34, 35–46, 98; symbolist criticism of, 35–43; symbolist influences on, 30, 110–112; in translation, 11, 116; in the USSR, 116

Pisarev, Dmitri, 26

Plot, 63–71; Aristotelian categories, 51, 68, 72; macro, 63–67; micro, 63, 68–71; in *TPD*, 63–71, 114

Pobedonostsev, Konstantin, 13–14, 15, 18, 20, 22, 23, 26; educational policies, 14–20

Possessed, The (Dostoevsky), 52, 99

Proust, Marcel, 47, 50

Pushkin, A.S., 17, 18, 26, 69, 85, 87–88, 90, 115

Rabinowitz, Stanley, 116–117

Radical critics, 18, 26

Realism, 47–50

Rech' (Speech), 37, 121 n 37

Red and the Black, The (Stendhal), 48–49

Religion in *TPD*, 101, 104–105; *see also* Peredonovism and religion

Revolutionary school of fiction, 27, 31

Russian Orthodox Church, 14, 28, 30, 39

Russian symbolist movement, 12, 26, 27–34, 35, 39, 47, 108–109, 112, 117; dualism, 29–30, 109, 111; generational theory of, 108; in politics, 30; religious wing of, 29, 37; role of the artist in, 30, 31, 112; and romanticism, 30–31; sources, 28–29; subgroups, 29; *see also* Neo-romanticism

This book forms part of the *Studies of the Harriman Institute*, successor to:

Studies of the Russian Institute

Abram Bergson, *Soviet National Income in 1937* (1953).

Ernest J. Simmons, Jr., ed., *Through the Glass of Soviet Literature: Views of Russian Society* (1953).

Thad Paul Alton, *Polish Postwar Economy* (1954).

David Granick, *Management of the Industrial Firm in the USSR: A Study in Soviet Economic Planning* (1954).

Allen S. Whiting, *Soviet Policies in China, 1917–1924* (1954).

George S.N. Luckyj, *Literary Politics in the Soviet Ukraine, 1917–1934* (1956).

Michael Boro Petrovich, *The Emergence of Russian Panslavism, 1856–1870* (1956).

Thomas Taylor Hammond, *Lenin on Trade Unions and Revolution, 1893–1917* (1956).

David Marshall Lang, *The Last Years of the Georgian Monarchy, 1658–1832* (1957).

James William Morley, *The Japanese Thrust into Siberia, 1918* (1957).

Alexander G. Park, *Bolshevism in Turkestan, 1917–1927* (1957).

Herbert Marcuse, *Soviet Marxism: A Critical Analysis* (1958).

Charles B. McLane, *Soviet Policy and the Chinese Communists, 1931–1946* (1958).

Oliver H. Radkey, *The Agrarian Foes of Bolshevism: Promise and Defeat of the Russian Socialist Revolutionaries, February to October, 1917* (1958).

Ralph Talcott Fisher, Jr., *Pattern for Soviet Youth: A Study of the Congresses of the Komsomol, 1918–1954* (1959).

Alfred Erich Senn, *The Emergence of Modern Lithuania* (1959).

Elliot R. Goodman, *The Soviet Design for a World State* (1960).

John N. Hazard, *Settling Disputes in Soviet Society: The Formative Years of Legal Institutions* (1960).

David Joravsky, *Soviet Marxism and Natural Science, 1917–1932* (1961).

Maurice Friedberg, *Russian Classics in Soviet Jackets* (1962).

Alfred J. Rieber, *Stalin and the French Communist Party, 1941–1947* (1962).

Theodore K. Von Laue, *Sergei Witte and the Industrialization of Russia* (1962).

John A. Armstrong, *Ukrainian Nationalism* (1963).

Oliver H. Radkey, *The Sickle under the Hammer: The Russian Socialist Revolutionaries in the Early Months of Soviet Rule* (1963).

Kermit E. McKenzie, *Comintern and World Revolution, 1928–1943: The Shaping of Doctrine* (1964).

Harvey L. Dyck, *Weimar Germany and Soviet Russia, 1926–1933: A Study in Diplomatic Instability* (1966).

(Above titles published by Columbia University Press.)

Harold J. Noah, *Financing Soviet Schools* (Teachers College, 1966).

John M. Thompson, *Russia, Bolshevism, and the Versailles Peace* (Princeton, 1966).

Paul Avrich, *The Russian Anarchists* (Princeton, 1967).

Loren R. Graham, *The Soviet Academy of Sciences and the Communist Party, 1927–1932* (Princeton, 1967).

Robert A. Maguire, *Red Virgin Soil: Soviet Literature in the 1920's* (Princeton, 1968).

T.H. Rigby, *Communist Party Membership in the U.S.S.R., 1917–1967* (Princeton, 1968).

Richard T. De George, *Soviet Ethics and Morality* (University of Michigan, 1969).

Jonathan Frankel, *Vladimir Akimov on the Dilemmas of Russian Marxism, 1895–1903* (Cambridge, 1969).

William Zimmerman, *Soviet Perspectives on International Relations, 1956–1967* (Princeton, 1969).

Paul Avrich, *Kronstadt, 1921* (Princeton, 1970).

Ezra Mendelsohn, *Class Struggle in the Pale: The Formative Years of the Jewish Workers' Movement in Tsarist Russia* (Cambridge, 1970).

Edward J. Brown, *The Proletarian Episode in Russian Literature* (Columbia, 1971).

Reginald E. Zelnik, *Labor and Society in Tsarist Russia: The Factory Workers of St. Petersburg, 1855–1870* (Stanford, 1971).

Patricia K. Grimsted, *Archives and Manuscript Repositories in the USSR: Moscow and Leningrad* (Princeton, 1972).

Ronald G. Suny, *The Baku Commune, 1917–1918* (Princeton, 1972).

Edward J. Brown, *Mayakovsky: A Poet in the Revolution* (Princeton, 1973).

Milton Ehre, *Oblomov and his Creator: The Life and Art of Ivan Goncharov* (Princeton, 1973).

Henry Krisch, *German Politics Under Soviet Occupation* (Columbia, 1974).

Henry W. Morton and Rudolph L. Tökés, eds., *Soviet Politics and Society in the 1970's* (Free Press, 1974).

William G. Rosenberg, *Liberals in the Russian Revolution* (Princeton, 1974).

Richard G. Robbins, Jr., *Famine in Russia, 1891–1892* (Columbia, 1975).

Vera Dunham, *In Stalin's Time: Middleclass Values in Soviet Fiction* (Cambridge, 1976).

Walter Sablinsky, *The Road to Bloody Sunday* (Princeton, 1976).

William Mills Todd III, *The Familiar Letter as a Literary Genre in the Age of Pushkin* (Princeton, 1976).

Elizabeth Valkenier, *Russian Realist Art. The State and Society: The Peredvizhniki and Their Tradition* (Ardis, 1977).

Susan Solomon, *The Soviet Agrarian Debate* (Westview, 1978).

Sheila Fitzpatrick, ed., *Cultural Revolution in Russia, 1928–1931* (Indiana, 1978).

Peter Solomon, *Soviet Criminologists and Criminal Policy: Specialists in Policy-Making* (Columbia, 1978).

Kendall E. Bailes, *Technology and Society under Lenin and Stalin: Origins of the Soviet Technical Intelligentsia, 1917-1941* (Princeton, 1978).

Leopold H. Haimson, ed., *The Politics of Rural Russia, 1905-1914* (Indiana, 1979).

Theodore H. Friedgut, *Political Participation in the USSR* (Princeton, 1979).

Sheila Fitzpatrick, *Education and Social Mobility in the Soviet Union, 1921-1934* (Cambridge, 1979).

Wesley Andrew Fisher, *The Soviet Marriage Market: Mate-Selection in Russia and the USSR* (Praeger, 1980).

Jonathan Frankel, *Prophecy and Politics: Socialism, Nationalism, and the Russian Jews, 1862-1917* (Cambridge, 1981).

Robin Feuer Miller, *Dostoevsky and the Idiot: Author, Narrator, and Reader* (Harvard, 1981).

Diane Koenker, *Moscow Workers and the 1917 Revolution* (Princeton, 1981).

Patricia K. Grimsted, *Archives and Manuscript Repositiories in the USSR: Estonia, Latvia, Lithuania, and Belorussia* (Princeton, 1981).

Ezra Mendelsohn, *Zionism in Poland: The Formative Years, 1915-1926* (Yale, 1982).

Hannes Adomeit, *Soviet Risk-Taking and Crisis Behavior* (George Allen & Unwin, 1982).

Seweryn Bialer and Thane Gustafson, eds., *Russia at the Crossroads: The 26th Congress of the CPSU* (George Allen & Unwin, 1982).

Roberta Thompson Manning, *The Crisis of the Old Order in Russia: Gentry and Government* (Princeton, 1983).

Andrew A. Durkin, *Sergei Aksakov and Russian Pastoral* (Rutgers, 1983).

Bruce Parrott, *Politics and Technology in the Soviet Union* (MIT Press, 1983).

Sarah Pratt, *Russian Metaphysical Romanticism: The Poetry of Tiutchev and Boratynskii* (Stanford, 1984).

Studies of the Harriman Institute

Elizabeth Kridl Valkenier, *The Soviet Union and the Third World: An Economic Bind* (Praeger, 1983).

John LeDonne, *Ruling Russia: Politics and Administration in the Age of Absolutism 1762-1796* (Princeton, 1984).